The Radical Alternative

Also by Jean-Jacques Servan-Schreiber

Lieutenant en Algérie
The American Challenge

JEAN-JACQUES SERVAN-SCHREIBER
AND MICHEL ALBERT

INTRODUCTION BY JOHN KENNETH GALBRAITH

The Radical
Alternative

TRANSLATED BY H. A. FIELDS

W · W · NORTON & COMPANY · INC ·
NEW YORK

Contents

Contents

Introduction

BY JOHN KENNETH GALBRAITH

Anyone who has written, however marginally, on politics
discovers how vivid is the interest in Europe and Japan in
American political ideas and experiment. It is an interest
which, to our disadvantage, we do not sufficiently recipro-
cate. In modern industrial society the problems in common
are far more important than the national differences. Nothing
is more interesting and suggestive and important than to see
these problems in the mirror the political leaders of other
countries hold up to them.

The most literate, most discussed, most abused, and quite
possibly the most interesting political leader in modern
France is Jean-Jacques Servan-Schreiber. After making a
name for himself as an opponent to the dead-end French policy in Algeria, then building a publication empire compa-

rable in magnitude (if not in viewpoint) to that of Henry Luce, then in his *The American Challenge* writing one of the great, best-selling economic and political tracts of modern times, he has plunged into French politics. His aim is to rejuvenate the French Radical Socialist Party, the custodian of the greatest (as we would say) liberal tradition in French politics but, in modern times, moribund in both spirit and program.

It is a book full of quick insights and flashing ideas. JJ-SS, as he is called, is not a man to dwell tediously on a point. He covers a myriad of matters—the rejuvenation of French corporations, the strategy for breaking the industrial power of the extensively hereditary industrial establishment, the reform of taxation, the decentralization of bureaucratic power, the program for agriculture, the liberalization and broadening of cultural life. On each he offers a lively and often brilliant suggestion. It is this which makes the book so useful to Americans. Here, almost at a glance, is the way this liveliest of French politicians sees the problem of government in the industrial and bureaucratic age. We see our problem better for seeing it through the eyes of this alert Frenchman. Knowledgeable Americans will have been told by head-shaking Frenchmen that JJ-SS is a quixotic figure, not a practical politician. This is true. No careful and shrewd, calculating, practical, professional politician would dream of writing a book like this. But then, no one with a grain of sense would dream of reading a book by such a politician. Only quixotic men think that ideas are important and have an influence on events.

Preface

From the distant reaches of the Orient we hear the chanting of the slogans of a new, grandiose, and terrible ambition. Mao, of whom history will possibly say that he alone proved capable of perceiving the immensity of our epoch, announces "a great revolutionary tempest, overturning heaven and earth." How? The little red book states it precisely and incisively: "Through man's submission to organization." Chinese Communism wishes to abolish man's individuality in order to bring about his collective happiness.

Here we are concerned with something else. We are concerned with the exact opposite.

Jeanne Hersch reminds us that political freedom is only "space opened to the soul, the protective form of actual freedom, which is the only human plenitude." We do not know how to make use of this fresh and fragile freedom. In truth we do not dare. Whether its aim is to reduce the gap between the hungry peoples of the world and those who are satiated or to restore quality to the life of industrial city-dwellers in the midst of their daily grind, Western policy is without perspective, without vitality, without ambition. Men submit to the force of circumstances and seek in it excuses for their resignation. We have become creatures and subjects of economic laws which have gained almost a monopoly over the essential features of our incomes, our environment, even our own roles. They control our destiny. We risk sacrificing our most precious values to their mechanical and immoral logic and our futures to their totalitarian tendencies. This is as true in the United States as in Europe. The economic processes we have learned from you have accelerated the threat.

The American Challenge was an attempt to warn against this immense danger. Necessarily partial and incomplete, it was intended to demonstrate that a nonindustrial, nonscientific, noncompetitive society can no longer take part in living history; that it is condemned to a status of submission. But industrial competitiveness and the capacity to innovate are only necessary preliminaries to freedom of political choice. A policy must have broader aims. The whole purpose of politics, what makes it noble, is the effort to assert control over our destiny. Today we have the knowledge and capacity to use science, technology, and economics to insure human freedom and to overcome the contradiction between what men are and what they want to be.

This is what we are aiming to achieve. But this does not mean we have a monopoly of the truth. The idea that any political party or program can save the world would be quite simply stupid, except for the fact that in the long run it corrupts the public mind. No one is entirely wrong. No one is entirely right. Both in democracy and in business enterprise, the association of complementary forces is the founda-

10

tion of effective action. We shall be careful in this book, as a matter of principle, not to be dogmatic in associating ourselves with the ardor of some or the wisdom of others.

Many men of good will expect from a political manifesto the key to all their problems. They anticipate it will bring heaven slightly closer to earth. But it is not only the limits of human reason that forbid such an undertaking. There is also respect for life and freedom. Infallible thoughts are closed systems. They postulate that history can only follow a single course and that everything has been predetermined. If this were the case, men, holding in their hands the booklet they have learned by heart, could only be the executors, spectators of their own destiny.

For our part, we have to understand that revolution consists precisely in transforming spectators into actors; in allowing the gushing forth of life, which is more complex, more fruitful, more creative than any theory or, if you like, any economic law.

For us, revolution means freedom to control and to shape our own future.

Acknowledgments

This work owes its origin to the political audacity of Maurice Faure, who, determined to bring about the revival of the French Radical Party when he took over its chairmanship in October 1969, asked me to contribute by preparing a program.

We were actively helped throughout the subsequent debates by the members of the Reform Commission.*

The study of France's economic stituation and the mea-

* This Commission, set up by the Chairman of the Radical Party, included, in addition to himself and myself, Pierre Brousse, Alain Chevalier, Michel Soulié, Robert Fabre, Auguste Pinton, Georges Bérard-Quélin, and also Felix Gaillard, who attended most of its meetings. The majority of its members, but not all of them, have approved this text. The text itself does not commit the Radical Party on matters of detail. It commits it certainly in spirit and as regards its proposals as a whole. But the only document whose every word is invested with the Party's authority is the thirty-page "Declaration" voted by the Wagram Congress.

sures which will be necessary to achieve our reforms—undertaken in some haste but based upon years of research—was the work of a team led by Michel Albert, Inspector of Finance. He is one of the pioneers of what is becoming the new economic thought. His analysis and insights were so important that it was natural to ask him to sign this work with me.

Finally, it is thanks to my friend Roger Priouret that our task was successfully accomplished. His vigilance, conviction, and balanced judgment allowed this project, from the first days of December 1969 to the last days of January 1970, to go as far as was reasonable—and not beyond.

I

From Submission
to Freedom

ONE

Today's Jungle:
The Economy

On the day Neil Armstrong walked on the moon, at that very moment, from one end of the earth to the other, in every time zone, at all hours of the day and night, in every town and village supplied with electricity, men, women, and children stopped, or woke up, to watch, and experience together, a first light step. It was like a new nativity. Never before had such a feeling of solidarity encompassed the earth. Does it not mean that from now on everything is possible? Does it not mean, if we wish, that the future of the next generation will be a fabulous future?

Meanwhile, two billion men—two-thirds of humanity, seem doomed to an animal destiny. They proliferate like insects. Once we hoped to integrate them fully into the human community through political independence and economic aid. This hope has been replaced by disillusioned indifference. Faced with the demographic deluge which threatens the so-called developed nations, two of them have already built up a rampart of nuclear weapons representing the equivalent of eighty tons of TNT per inhabitant of the planet. This, we are told by both of them, is owing to "the force of circumstances."

The force of circumstances: this must be the enemy. Whoever submits to it becomes a slave and prepares the chains for others. Whoever opposes it, and even revolts against it, does his duty as a man.

At the heart of this refusal is man himself. If he exists at all, it is primarily because he gradually overcame the jungle of nature which was oppressing and killing him. After centuries and centuries, his inventions finally have overcome the law of hunger and scarcity, first through industry, and then through the law of distances and physical force. From the first steam engine to the computer, there is still a world, crossed in a very few years by the triumphal progress of the creations of the mind. With the conquest of the moon, the laws of gravity have in their turn been thrown onto the scrap heap of those decrees of nature which man's marvelous contrivances have abolished. One of the great laws still defying him, apparently as immutable as the earth's rotation, has just been vanquished.

But while smashing his ancestral chains, industrial man was forging new ones. A new nature rose to face him: the economy itself. The two most important inventions since the end of World War II have been the nuclear weapon and sustained economic growth. Together they have changed the world. The first has completely overturned the equations of war and peace, as Khrushchev courageously admitted when he disowned Lenin's theories on the inevitability of wars. But even this is less important than the economic revolution. The regular increase in the economic product—averaging between 3 and 5 per cent a year in the industrial countries—means that henceforth a man can count upon his purchasing power to triple in the course of his active life, even without any professional promotion.

Since the beginning of humanity, man's purchasing power had remained almost constant and miserable. For centuries, economic scarcity made oppression and cruelty the cardinal principles of life in society. During the first Industrial Revolution of the nineteenth century, annual economic growth did not exceed 1 per cent a year, except in the United States. For long periods it was either minimal or negative. Thus, the annual per capita income of the French people in the fifteen years between 1924 and 1938 actually *fell* by 2 per cent.

The benefits of growth are not limited to material needs. The progress of freedom of thought and of political freedoms depends upon the people having sufficient income so as not to have to make Winston Churchill's choice "between freedom and a full stomach." A growing standard of living extends the margin of choice of the individual into the most varied fields, reflecting the growth of organizing intelligence. It is, from this point of view, a source of justifiable pride.

When we perceive from what hell economic growth has rescued us, we know, once and for all, that it must be a primary object of our cares. No one will be allowed to govern a free society if he is not clearly capable of handling and improving this new weapon. This is the First Commandment.

But it is only a starting point. Everything else still remains to be done. Man's fight—the political fight—must now be

19

carried further, into the new arena of the economy. Little time remains to win this fight. To free man from savage nature took thousands and thousands of years; to free man from the economy will be the task of a generation: our own.

Industrial societies, far from spreading equilibrium, serenity, and happiness, are seething cultures in which new types of frustrations, tensions, aggressiveness, and violence proliferate. While economies have grown beyond the wildest dreams of last century's visionaries, the most intensely felt needs of the people, which should have the highest priority, are not being met.

This is most obvious in Communist countries, where the economic system is based upon government choice, often arbitrary, imposed upon the whole population. In western countries, the distortion between what people really need and what they are actually offered is less marked but nevertheless important. Our basic needs, especially for food, are being progressively satisfied as a matter of course. Secondary needs, for industrial products, are stimulated by an entire system of external pressures linked to the apparatus of production; they tend to be more than satisfied. On the other hand, what economists call tertiary needs (services, equipment, education, town planning, information, transport, leisure, housing, etc.) remain largely undersatisfied, especially when their provision is the duty of the public authorities. Thus the gap between the possible and desirable constantly increases.

Liberal theory, which successfully implemented the first Industrial Revolution, is based upon the idea that real needs, expressed through the market, command production. Consumers decide and production adapts itself in order to execute the orders. "The consumer is in short the king . . . ," writes economist Paul Samuelson.

But as the process of development continues, the consumer-producer relationship tends to reverse itself and, in the absence of political will, to keep growth under control. The powerful apparatus of production adapts itself not only to society's needs, but also to its own imperatives. The capitalist economy is capable of invading everything, including private life (into which it now penetrates deeply and decisively through television). It can lead man to give up his soul in order to manufacture a humanity in its own image. The producer needs a consumer as his creature. He has to influence cultural life in order to modify behavior. His only hurdle is our own internal sanctuary, our intimate aspiration to reserve in our existence something which is ours and ours alone.

The demands of the economy tend to make of man a raw material to be exploited by industry. They require individuals who are not only wealthier, but conformist; they tend to create beings as empty as possible, vacuums into which the goods manufactured may find an outlet.

Thus, far from controlling the economy, man today runs the risk of becoming its slave, its object, being treated in accordance with the same laws of profitability it imposes on everything else. This reversal of the situation has led to new inequalities and threatens still more, which will replace those imposed by the long night of scarcity. It shows today all the features of a cumulative process. It is mutilating us already. From their very first years, our children, tender and vulnerable, are subjected to a mercantile interpretation of man and society. No longer do they learn their values from the family or the school. Industrial society exerts a continual pressure on a child as soon as he can see and hear.

The adult is the consumer-producer who, by means of his gifts, education, and job, plies a trade which brings him an income. In the past, the wealth of the privileged generated for them a life of grace, a sense of security, and a certain degree of freedom. Today it only increases the attraction of the material goods for the consumer. The rising standard of living, even though it satisfies material needs, thus becomes a source of irritation and growing frustration, the size of which can be measured by noting that consumer credit is rising much more rapidly than incomes. As people become richer, necessities tend to become increasingly more exacting, and needs become more acute. It is a form of "psychological pauperization." Parodoxically, dissatisfaction increases. It has to, in any case, in order to offer the machine—which demands it—increasingly wider outlets. The process requires that the consumer should receive, at the same time, both an increased income and all the symbols which place him in a situation of subjective penury. Professor John Kenneth Galbraith goes as far as to say: "The big firm molds the attitudes of society in accordance with its own needs. What passes for a valid social objective is very often only a reflection of the aims of the large corporations and the managers of the technostructure."

The further man as a buyer departs from elementary physical needs, the easier it becomes to persuade and condition him. The big firms are rapidly accentuating this tendency today by growing to world size. They and they alone can thus adjust their strategy to the entire planet, rid themselves of national impediments and laws, while the public authorities are rapidly losing the means of controlling the automatism of the economy. The whole industrial system, which should be an instrument in the service of mankind, tends to become the norm, in terms of which men have to adapt their behavior, their social relationships, and even their selves. This submission of man to the laws of the economy is the second fundamental fact of our present situation.

Growth remains the major phenomenon from the point

of view of history: it is the irreplaceable lever. Its consequences, its disequilibriums, its injustices may be judged secondly in relation to history. But for political man today, the reverse is true.

The reason is that the mechanisms of growth are continually improving and being improved. One after the other, industrial societies are learning how to operate them. But the restraints which economic laws involve are hardly taken into account, still less mastered. A political plan is therefore required whose main principle is to free man from the ravages of the economy and whose main objective is to rescue him, from this new inevitable fate.

For us it is unacceptable to argue, as many do, that nothing can be done. "We can't help it, it's progress" Each year, hundreds of thousands of perplexed farm workers, isolated shopkeepers, despised tradesmen, insufficiently skilled workmen, poorly trained research workers, miserably pensioned-off old men , women tired out by prolonged household cares face inactivity and the advent of poverty with the coming of old age. They are uprooted and tortured by the forward march of economy. Is this "the law of progress"? Unemployment does not just affect the poor and untrained. It has hit the scientific community, the shipbuilders, the miners. Can they who are doing well in productive employment fail to notice that, in their turn, they too will be caught and condemned to misery one day if they allow this immoral law to operate against its weakest victims?

Who therefore will organize conscious and rational political action? This is the question the Radicals in France, and liberals in other nations, are asking themselves. And they address this question on behalf of those who suffer because of progress to those who share a common concern with them.

From Submission to Freedom

These immoral consequences of economic progress are presented to us as a new inevitable fate against which our societies can do nothing. This abdication of policy in face of the economy, which is the mark of those in power today, is exceedingly dangerous. It could cost us our very existence.

One sign of this in Europe is the lazy and unquestioning acceptance of an economic and cultural model imported from abroad, that of the United States. The true challenge of scientific progress for European countries consists, on the other hand, in being inventive for ourselves. We must resist servile imitation, not by negating progress, which could only lead us to still more dependence upon the United States, but by formulating and implementing a plan that relates man to his environment in ways the United States has not done.

There are strong moral reasons favoring a diversity of cultures. But even apart from them, the economic facts of contemporary life show that a country cannot develop by copying models invented elsewhere which are necessarily adapted to other traditions and other mentalities.

In France today, for example, there is a taste for discussion, an understanding of wider issues, an aspiration for a better life, whose traditional and essentially true theme of the "just measure" is very suggestive. This is the sort of theory that must be integrated, in the name of economic development itself, in any plan for evolution. This is true for every country and for every region within a country. The just and natural control of the modern economy can lead to the cultural diversity, not to uniformity.

As long as economics instead of politics is in control, a subjectively accepted cultural framework will be imposed upon an objectively questionable economic framework. Man's training, his culture, his way of life, his destiny will

24

continue to be treated as factors of production. We must recognize the dangers inherent in the re-education of man into a raw material. He is educated and trained for output. He is classified according to whether he is profitworthy or not. He is considered as "depreciated"—the word itself is suggestive—as he becomes less profitworthy. He is rejected when he ceases to be profitworthy. This is the life men in industrial societies are living. The Radical plan aims to reverse its course.

Before examining more closely those who are rejected and sacrificed by the law of progress because they are weakest, let us examine the fate of those it favors. The senior officials, those with the highest incomes, the modern managers— what sort of happiness do they achieve? What sort of life do they lead? Galbraith writes: "The manager is generally proud to let his firm absorb nearly all the energy of his waking hours. Everything else, including his family, politics and even drinking or sex—everything else is secondary." The French word for work, *travail*, is linked through its etymology to the notion of torture. It comes from *tripalium*, an instrument of torture comprising three stakes. In French maternity hospitals, the room where the future mother suffers and weeps bears the name of "labor room" (*salle de travail*). What an inversion it is to see work becoming, under our very eyes, the main, and often the only, center of interest in the life of those referred to as senior managers!

There is also the danger that business activity tends, through diversification, to separate the men of the industrial age into two categories, almost two races. The managers, those who participate in the great economic game and enjoy income from capital, live a life of business, making their fortunes and our history—just as the patricians of Rome used to live a life of politics. They fix the scale of values. But what values? They are bored when they are not working. No wonder in the United States, upper-middle-class husbands experience such a high rate of divorce and lose touch with their own children. The other workers, the plebeians, the yokels of the new society, are bored and miserable at their work. Their leisure activities are often poor and derisory.

The progress that has been made in management techniques, particularly in the development of cost accounting, adds to this inequality. As these techniques become more detailed, more computerized, the marginal efficiency of each individual in the circuit of production at every level becomes better known. And since it varies from zero to infinity, it follows automatically that the range of incomes itself tends to become disproportionately wide. Thus, increasing economic rationality brings with it the increased risk of human injustice.

As time goes by, the level of demands imposed upon individuals by the rigors of progress becomes higher. In a "poorly constructed" system, man can always believe it is the system which is wrong. In a rationalized social organization where the economy is the master, it is necessarily the man who is wrong and maladjusted. Louis Armand,[1] a staunch advocate of economic growth but of a growth which would remain human, sums up the parallel with this image:

In countries like France and Italy, one of the favorite outdoor games is bowls (*pétanque*). It can be played on any dirt or grassy surface. The man who loses at bowls can always blame the unevenness of the ground or defects in his ball. This permits unending discussions and maintains friendships in the Mediterranean countries. But where there is a well-laid-out bowling alley, clean, flat, uniform, and

[1] Scientist, author, member of the Académie Française (1963), former president of the French National Railroad (1955), president of Westinghouse-Europe.

26

rational, the man who loses can only blame himself. All he can do is get a complex about it, or go drinking.

The urban centers of industrial society offer living illustrations of this parable. People go mad. The increase in mental disorders, the need to use tranquilizers, sleeping pills, stimulants, and euphorizers are signs—and there are millions of them—of the profound internal disturbances caused by the alienation of man by the industrial system. The German chemical industry, the most sophisticated in Europe, has invented 662 brands of sleeping pills. They are all consumed.

What kind of society is this which gives abundantly to its favorites the external symbols of happiness, but where the supreme luxury for the princes of industry—who enjoy weekend jet flights, twice-weekly golf games, safaris in Kenya, rest cures in Switzerland, and winter holidays in the Caribbean—is to be able to manage without tranquilizers? Paranoia, the characteristic neurosis of our time, is a neurosis of frustration. The sufferer believes he is not receiving his due from society. Whatever his standard of living, he is in a situation of objective penury. Now, writes François Bloch-Lainé,[2] "It is becoming less and less natural to be adapted, or to remain adapted."

Let us question the wives of senior managers in industrial corporations: the advance witnesses of life in the future. Thanks to their improved standard of living, do your husbands have more or less work to do than ten years ago? Do they have more or less time available for family life? To read, to relax with you? Using the economists' own expression in its true meaning, what becomes of their capacity for enjoyment of life? Were an industrial organization to

[2] President of the Crédit Lyonnais, one of the first French State Banks; author of the well-known book on industrial reform *Pour une réforme de l'entreprise.*

27

be content with such a low return, its output itself would be condemned.

Even those who believe they are really well off and who are still obsessed by the "Communist menace" (a convenient alibi to be brandished for the perpetuation of privileges and social barriers) should realize before it is too late that they are threatened from within by a far more real evil.

Finding too few of the magic virtues attributed by advertising to his actual acquisitions, the buyer is led to destroy them or to forget them and immediately starts searching for others. He is searching for an illusion. Like one of Beckett's characters, his existence serves only to fill a great garbage can with the cheap finery in which his personality has dissolved. And this imbalance in favor of industrial products, diversified ad infinitum, to the detriment of goods and service of a collective nature, revives inequalities and worsens social divisions. The rich man suffers less from the shortage of hospitals: private clinics always have room. The rich man can avoid the drawbacks of too few schools or the shortage of equipment in public establishments: he creates private schools and gives them the necessary financial backing. The rich man can dodge peak-hour traffic jams and jam-packed public transport vehicles: he arrives at his office and leaves at the times he chooses.

But very few have this kind of money and flexibility. As for the others, the huge majority of wage and salary earners ranging up to top levels, the shortcomings of collective goods and services are today an essential factor of frustration and tension within society. According to a poll taken by a French polling organization, 54 per cent of the population of Paris—which is the subject of envy of the rest of France —would, if it could, leave Paris "to go and live elsewhere." But where?

The industrial system which is in control and the politicians which are its servants instead of its masters wildly over-estimate certain human values and amputates others; its logic is that of uniformity. The more it spreads, the more the domination of the great multinational corporation is asserted, and the more the law of progress—ill-adapted, ill-mastered, ill-controlled—attacks diversity and consequently humanity. This is one of the great failures of modern politics.

We have therefore to conceive another policy, a new alliance between the vital pulses which make man himself and the intellectual norms which are necessary for the rational conduct of the economy. Desirable as it may be, from the standpoint of progress, that the material infrastructure of societies should become increasingly homogeneous and spread rapidly throughout the world, it is just as desirable that this evolution should be associated with a renaissance of society and culture. This is a political task.

The conclusion to which we are led by this outline of our contemporary society, its laws, and its tendencies, is that we are living in a world that is insufficiently politicized. It is not being directed by a clear awareness of the objectives to be attained and the means needed to attain them. We should remember the philosophical question asked by Jean-Jacques Rousseau: "Nature gives us only too many needs. And it is a great imprudence to say the least to multiply them needlessly, and thus place one's soul in even greater dependency. It is not without reason that Socrates, looking at a shop display, congratulated himself that he had no need of any of that."

At the time Mme. Leprince de Beaumont expressed the opposite view in the following terms: "A man without any needs, and consequently without any desires, would be a dolt. It is sentiment which makes us happy. A sentiment implies, or supposes, an object corresponding to it. This object

29

excites desires. These desires and then the means of satisfying them are the very sources of happiness."

In the end, industrial societies believe themselves excused from making a choice. They have opted in favor of the position taken by Mme. Leprince de Beaumont against Rousseau. But they have done so by unconsciously sacrificing a large number of those higher aspirations which form part of human needs.

Thus aggressiveness and violence, which our entire history—the history of scarcity—have engraved in the very heart of politics, remain the mainspring and the effect of progress. The modern form of violence is economics.

Can one nourish the bold ambition of strengthening the mechanisms of the growth economy, guarantors of the constant rise in the standard of living, while also abstracting man from this process, so that in the end the same laws of profitworthiness no longer apply to him? This is our conviction. It will be our plan.

The evolution of society and of social relationships can thus be summed up in three essential stages:

1. *The stage of coercion: nature in power.* This stretched from the very origin of life to the Industrial Revolution of the last century. Societies were narrowly hierarchical, human activity was based upon the fear of penalties and social sanctions. These societies of coercion, those of yesterday and those of today, possess every defect. Intolerant and inefficient, they impose, in all fields, subjection to a quasi-military discipline.

2. *The stage of liberalism: economics in power.* Each one working in his own interest, the organized interplay of oppositions between individuals and classes which allows a certain collective well-being to be attained. But such a social regime institutes a necessary domination of the strong over the weak; and by treating man essentially in accordance

with economic laws, it gives a scant share to the truly human values of solidarity, equality and generosity.

3. *The stage of politics: man in power.* This is the one we have to reach. We want man to gradually become reconciled with himself through creative labor and with others by sharing in disinterested activities. This would mean, in the style of Teilhard de Chardin, aiming at a point omega on the horizon where, thanks to the continual improvement of social organization and an incessant effort on himself, each person would find, in accordance with his vocation, a certain capacity to bloom.

It is clear that this diagram of evolution is less descriptive than normative. It expresses less a philosophy of history than a hierarchy of human values which has to guide our efforts.

Saint-Simon [3] imagined that industrial progress would lead automatically to a domestication of politics: he was wrong. So was Auguste Comte. New inequalities arise and multiply. Our society, one of economics, is subjected in its turn, just like savage societies, to scourges and elementary needs. In the so-called cities of abundance, noise wears down, asphyxia chokes, nerves crack, beings search every evening for nonexistent shelter. It was not Voltaire or Rousseau who said: "Hell is other people," but Jean-Paul Sartre —our contemporary. And which of us, one day, has not uttered this accusation?

Those who by instinct find themselves, or wish to be, on the side of the weakest know that they have once again something to do. Everything to do. It will not be easy. The human spirit vacillates in front of difficulty. However, we must try; this is the essential role of political man.

[3] Claude-Henri de Rouvroy, Count de Saint-Simon (1760–1825). Nineteenth-century apostle of industrial development.

TWO

The Eternal Order
of Things

Forget about the golden age, once and for all. It never existed. Our past, our entire past, is horrible. History books are still essentially fairy-tales about the powerful. The entire history of man, including our fathers' generation—that of Hitler and Stalin—unfolded in a universe of penury and under the rule of the laws of scarcity.

If economic growth is erecting for us a disappointing and unharmonious city; if the political challenge of the end of this century is to assume power over the economy; if we are dissatisfied and, in solidarity with the weakest, resolved to propose real changes, then at least let us not make the mistake of so many intellectuals and young people who, following Proudhon [1] ("Poverty is good and we must consider it as the principle of our liveliness"), wish to believe that material austerity can constitute the basis of a social morality.

Let us look at actual history, not that which conquerors made their flatterers write and which school children are still learning, but that which the peoples of the world have written in silence, with their suffering, their ignorance, and their tears. This is the object lesson which can illuminate our proposals.

The Third World has always lived with the misery of permanent death, but only yesterday did the men who make history, those belonging to the countries that have finally emerged from scarcity, notice it. The industrial countries have only recently become acutely aware of the fundamental fact that two-thirds of our contemporaries are still living in such a state of underdevelopment that their food ration is below the physiological minimum. It is like a revelation. Had not Africa, Asia, and Latin America been considered for centuries as huge reserves of wealth? From Marco Polo to Lyautey, navigators and colonists, explorers and merchants discovered "fabulous treasures," where suddenly we ourselves can only see immense misery. The reality is what we see today. The other was a mirage or, at best, window dressing.

In any case, what is astonishing is not that two-thirds of humanity is still hungry, but rather that one-third is well fed. This is the radically new phenomenon—the one which allows us to distinguish the two parts of history: the first characterized by fixity of techniques and the permanence of scarcity; the second, the one we are living in, marked by the

[1] Pierre-Joseph Proudhon (1809–1865). Philosopher, creator of French Socialism, defender of federalism.

accelerated progress of scientific techniques and, something which is entirely new, continuous economic growth.

At the time of the French Revolution, the average wage of a worker in France represented only 1,800 calories a day, whereas the physiological minimum is around 3,000. Yet France of that time was, with England, the most developed country in the world. Up to our time, no people at any moment in history had ever succeeded in producing a quantity of goods to ensure, in a continuous manner, to the whole of its population, a food supply coping with simple elementary physiological needs. That is the main point of our history. No prior "civilization" was ever able to utilize the whole complex of methods which have allowed agriculture to increase its productivity (fertilizers, seeds, traction). The empires of the ancient world and the Renaissance created incontestable progress in the military, administrative, judicial, and artistic fields; none of them transformed the techniques of production. The most famous one, the Roman Empire, did not in fact exploit new inventions. The wealth of the "divine city" did not come from productivity, but from the plunder of manpower and treasure in the countries comprising, or neighboring, the empire.

The most ancient biblical testimony, like the present-day motto of the Workers' International, shows that from the furthest antiquity to the present day, bread, the humble loaf of bread, remained the symbol of a good human food supply. It was the only food that could be produced on a mass scale, and even then only barely.

Modern man has just now learned simultaneously to increase his productivity and to limit his offspring: two ways to begin to escape from inevitable fate. Our ancestors were ignorant of both. It is not that man did not find ingenious ways to fight off demographic danger. He used the most

34

varied and cruel means. Infanticide was one of the most
stable social institutions. Witness the history of famous sur-
vivors, from Moses to Romulus. In Japan, today the champ-
ion of modern productivity, the Tokugawa Shoguns' special
police up until one hundred years ago, would regularly, on
orders from the Emperor, chop off the heads of newborn
babies in families judged to be too large. And according to
modern sociologists, the main function of the dreary succession of wars in world history was to ward off the danger
of human proliferation in an economically closed and im-
mobile world.

Nature itself contributed, in dreadful fashion. Before the
Industrial Revolution, one child out of three died in its
first year, apart from those who died at birth. For those who
survived, the average life-span in Europe a century ago—
like that of India today—was only twenty-five years. Now it
is between sixty and seventy years.

In addition to natural mortality and the ravages of wars,
epidemics took care of the remainder. The two great waves
of the Black Plague each killed in their time one-third of the
known population of Christendom.

Taine [2] writes: "The people are like a man walking
through a pond with water up to his mouth. At the least
dip of the ground, at the least wave, he loses his foothold,
goes under and chokes." This was our situation the day before yesterday. It is still true today for two-thirds of humanity. In comparison with this permanent scarcity, the
"civilizations" have been only a series of fugitive waves on
the surface of the life of the peoples.

Thus the human adventure was dominated from begin-

[2] Hippolyte Taine (1828–1893). Conservative historian, philosopher, and
critic; author of the well-known book *Les origines de la France con-
temporaine.*

ning to end by the phenomenon of scarcity: the huge majority of men lived a life of calamity, truncated in its content as well as in its length.

Since the timid and pale dawn of economic growth in the last century, the length of the working week has, on average, been reduced by nearly half. In the main industrialized countries, the rise in the standard of living has been in the ratio of 1 to 3. But it is only since 1945 that economic growth really took off, beginning with the United States of America and moving out in concentric waves. It had taken three-quarters of a century (1880–1953) for productivity to double in France. It then doubled once again within ten years. In those countries capable of administering their growth, it is due to treble in the next twenty years and average working time at the end of the century will be one day in two.[3]

This economic development is transforming all aspects of human societies. In all fields, man's traditional situation in the face of the nature of things is becoming reversed. A static economy generates the eternal "Josephian" cycle [4]— the succession of years of the fat kine and years of the lean kine, leaving man a stranger to the notion of progress. One can thus understand why, from Virgil to Milton, all golden ages, all paradises lost were situated in the past: *in illo tempore*. This conception is at the heart of Judaeo-Christian thought. In the Old Testament, the idea of salvation is associated with the idea of a return to the poverty of the patriarchal era. On Ascension Day, the Apostles ask Christ: "Lord, wilt thou at this time *restore again* the kingdom to Israel?"

The social relationships which today pervade our life are inherited from the static economy, the one in which, as Col-

[3] See Jean Fourastié, *The Great Hope of the Twentieth Century.*
[4] Pierre Moussa, *The Proletarian Nations.*

bert [5] puts it: "What we give to some, we take from others." Who, in any case, does not continue to behave as though this were true?

And this also explains some essential traits of our society, especially the part played by hierarchies. Luxury and destitution go together. In a developed economy, wealth proceeds from a collective creation, but in a more-or-less static economy, it cannot spring from anything other than a predatory action exercised by the strong over the weak.

Today, the output of the American farmer is on average twenty times higher than that of the African peasant. He knows how to apply to the soil a whole range of treatments and techniques which, while reducing his own effort, allow him to multiply natural fecundity. Not only has he mastered nature, but he has also created goods which, without him, without his action, would never have existed.

If this is true of agriculture, where natural factors continue to play a very important part, it is truer still in other fields of economic activity. Production and creation have become synonymous. That is a major historic change. The African peasant, like yesterday's European man, is incapable of acting on the physical factors of his environment. He can only increase the quantity of his goods by taking them from other members of society. Like the player in a zero-sum game, he is unable to satisfy his needs, far less enrich himself, except at someone else's expense.

In moving from scarcity to creation, men have not only transformed their attitude towards nature, but have acquired the capacity, if they so desire, to modify their respective positions as regards each other. They are called upon to assert their solidarity: developed economies have, as distinctive characteristics, a complexity, a complementary nature, and an interdependence. Interdependence and economic progress

[5] Jean-Baptiste Colbert (1619–1683). Finance minister under Louis XIV.

go hand in hand. The complexity of the networks of exchanges increases while each one of their elements becomes increasingly vital. In an age of electric power stations, mass transit and far-flung food distribution, the well-being of each single man is becoming increasingly dependent upon the activity of others.

The growing interdependence of the nations, the activity of the sciences, the never-ending innovations which are extending the economy's spatial and temporal framework—all are creating a new universe, in which the number of persons fulfilling a given function continually decreases in comparison to the number of persons benefiting from it.

Certainly, the contrast between a society of scarcity and a society of creation is not absolute from the point of view of the sources of wealth. The fact that developed economies need a whole new network of interdependency does not by itself lead to the withering away of antagonism and conflict. On the contrary, the class struggle has been, through its very ambiguity, a powerful factor in economic development. By forcibly extracting pay rises, the working-class forces have constantly stimulated increasing productivity and thus allowed innovations to be introduced, creating new profits of which the proportion reinvested is the mainspring of general prosperity.

But all these remarks are of limited historical importance alongside the fact that technological progress allows the creation of a supplement of wealth which can benefit the entire productive collectivity, independently of any improvement of its distribution among its verious members. Moral considerations command us to transform this distribution as well. But the fact remains that it is creation which is the fundamental phenomenon. It changes the fundamental facts upon which immutable theories of power and political con-

38

struction had been based. We can already see how this new phenomenon has destroyed certain elements of Marxist theory.[6] But more important, it calls for, and allows, the destruction of what used to appear, and still appears today, to be natural and necessary: hierarchical oppression.

For it is obvious that scarcity, and scarcity alone, imposed the rigor of hierarchies:

Hierarchies within the family. Strict family hierarchies are preserved in economies with low productivity, or in those whose mental evolution has not yet followed their economic evolution. The history of the condition of the female sex, in our society in particular, is nothing more than the exploitation of weakness by strength.

Professional hierarchies. In scarcity societies and those which are their political heirs, birth, as we shall show, determines one's destiny. The various trades and professions are assigned a quasi-intangible place on the rungs of social consideration. Up to the Industrial Revolution, the old class system was absolutely immutable. Regardless of his talent, Haydn wore the livery of the Esterhazys all his life, and Mozart learned the hard way what it meant to violate taboos when claiming the right to choose his own masters.

Social hierarchies. Despite the development of industrial society, very few people succeed in overcoming the obstacles of social stratification. This is far less true in the United States than in Europe, which is one important explanation for America's progress. In Europe, everything was designed, in law and in custom, to exaggerate inequalities, and to oppose, as Fourier [7] puts it, "the ascending chain of hatreds and the descending chain of contempts." The logic of the "per-

[6] We shall return to this argument in chapter three when analyzing links between growth, reform, and revolution.

[7] Charles Fourier (1772–1837). Utopian Socialist.

39

sistent hatreds" generated by scarcity requires furthermore that any deviation should be repressed. For this reason, capital punishment was an important feature of scarcity societies. Joseph de Maistre [8] did not surprise anyone when he affirmed: 'Society can exist only thanks to the hangman." During the *belle époque* of the Flemish Masters, blood used to flow once a week in the great square of Bruges, and the bodies of those executed used to be left hanging for months from the belfries in front of the eyes of prudish nuns.

Thus, it is not coincidence, but rather a sign of the evolution of the species, that the first European country to have abolished the death penalty was Holland, which, of all the Common Market countries, is the most enterprising in trade, the most open to international exchanges, and the most egalitarian from the point of view of income distribution. The last death sentence in Sweden dates back to 1910. Then the death penalty was abolished. Brutality in social relationships is linked to scarcity and what remains of it. The fact that in Europe, Portugal, Spain, and France alone have kept the death penalty is not without significance.

Finally, the history of scarcity has bequeathed to us, in the political field, archetypes which are all based, fundamentally, on the model of military organization. For in order that the privileged classes should be able to protect themselves and resist internal revolt—as well as outside aggression—they had to equip themselves with unity of command and to organize themselves in accordance with a pyramidal structure. Warfare leads to political subordination, which is the rampart of economic privileges. In these conditions, the idea of a social contract was only part of the apparatus of self-justification used by the ruling classes. When the danger of internal tensions was less acute, it would be quickly replaced by the threat of external covetousness. In the midst of pov-

[8] (1753–1821). Polemical writer, advocate of absolute monarchy.

erty, the doors to abundance opened only to those who had power. Only war was productive.

No nation understood this better than France—and we are still paying for it. Unity of command, so necessary to the efficiency of armies, was also the key to civil power. "All war-like geniuses like centralization and all centralizing geniuses like war," noted de Tocqueville.

The same implacable mechanisms lead from scarcity to inequality, from inequality to sovereignty, from sovereignty to war. The more powerful one is, the richer one is. The richer one is, the more one is envied. As soon as one stops advancing, one retreats. . . . It is therefore necessary to be always stronger, always the strongest.

Thus politics has never been anything other than a negation, an inversion of human values. How could Caesar compound with God? What state ever proved capable of ensuring its continued existence by depriving itself of the glory of arms? Machiavelli summed it all up: "War, and the institutions and rules concerning it, are the only object to which a Prince must devote his thoughts; it is the true profession of whoever rules." A shrewd humanist, he had nourished himself with the milk of antiquity, and no one better than he was able to express the determinism with which underdevelopment has marked politics.

If politics never was moral, it is because a social "morality" of scarcity is inconceivable. That is how Charles de Gaulle's disillusioned remark must be understood: "Evangelical perfection does not lead to Empire. The man of action can hardly be conceived without a heavy dose of selfishness, pride, harshness and craft." A mere echo of Machiavelli, and of eternity.

Industrial society, moving over from scarcity to growth, gradually snatched everything away from nature: knowledge, technology, production, and even gravity. Everything, that is, except politics, which is still a motionless part of the animal kingdom within the human kingdom.

Can politics in its turn enter into history? Will political man be able to remold the artificial constraints of this "second nature," economics, in order to turn them into a supportive framework? This is part of our mission.

The mainsprings of social life have really been distrust and contempt on the one hand, and civil, military, or religious fear on the other. The imperious nature of the hierarchy has created an extreme inequality which men have considered to be natural. From this derives the importance of the principle of heredity, which remains so deeply rooted in European societies; the prevalence of secrecy and lies, which are almost institutional, both in our business firms and in our politics; and the acknowledged superiority of a social organization founded upon castes and centralization.

In past centuries, this order of things has been sanctified by calling it either the divine will or the decrees of nature. It has always appeared normal that each man was to occupy within society a place in accordance with his birth; that social life was inconceivable except in separative classes; and that discipline was the very principle of collective efficiency. Was not all this in accordance with what, even today, is referred to as common sense?

It must have taken immense generosity of mind, courage, and strength for those first reformers—Socialists and Radicals—to dare to begin to attack this structure, point by point. The impetus which we shall need to snatch away from economics what they themselves snatched away from nature can be found in what they did. The inspiration of their work, the lesson of their failures, the reasons for their success can be a useful text for us. They proved that progress is based, necessarily, on a philosophy entirely different from this respect for the "nature of things" which characterizes the conservatives of all periods.

THREE

Reform, Instrument of Revolution

Reform or revolution? The quarrel enlivens the recollections of old militants, the philosophical debates at academies, and the drawing-room conversations of the liberals. In the United States, it is the chief issue by which young people still committed to the democratic system try to hold the initiative against violence as a political tool. Economics and history teach us, however, that reality is expressed in other terms.

According to current political jargon, just about everything is now called a reform. Is the scale of charges for public services being modified? A reform. Is there an awareness of the need to change the system of financing social security? A reform. Are business firms going to be allowed to recover

44

part of their taxes in order to distribute them to third parties? A reform. The term is applied to measures aimed at balancing the budget, stabilizing the currency, reducing the period of military service, developing telephone services and motorways, and so forth. Much that is presented as great reform is merely a modification indispensable for improved administration.

While the improvement of efficiency in the interest of growth is essential, it is not reform. If reform is what transforms the nature of the social contract, the only true reform is a revolutionary one. And if revolution is supposed to be a mutation towards progress, the industrial countries have learned by and large not to confuse it any more with regression by violence.

Jean Boissonnat [1] wrote: "In a developed industrial society, I am not certain that the revolution could choose any other road than reformism. The trade-union member will no longer confuse the revolutionary talk of former times with the action which effectively, and even radically, transforms today's reality. In the final analysis, there is nothing more revolutionary than reformism taken seriously."

With those words was written the history of the first mutation which, with the beginnings of growth, snatched man away from the fatalities of the eternal order of things. This history does not supply us with any decalogue or totalitarian doctrine; but it teaches us a method, and some lessons.

At a time when we have to undertake a new mutation designed to liberate man, it is useful to see how the original Radicals and Socialists in France began their attack on the political structure inherited from the world of scarcity. The Radicals were the first truly reformist political party in France. Many of the measures that William Jennings Bryan,

[1] Journalist; editor-in-chief of *Expansion*, the best-known French economic magazine.

Woodrow Wilson, and the two Roosevelts fought for in the United States had already been brought into the political arena by the French Radicals. We must keep in mind the reasons for their successes, and their failures, and especially the arguments invoked by conservatives to spread the fear of reform among the people by showing, with every appearance of competence and wisdom, the risks involved in the disintegration of the social order.

The freedoms with which we are familiar and which now appear indefeasible seem to date from very far back in history; we often believe they were born with the declaration of the Rights of Man proclaimed on August 26, 1789. But when we look a little closer, we see that the revolutionary years during which the Rights of Man were effectively enforced were only a microscopic interlude. They were not only fleeting but debatable: can one speak of the Rights of Man under the Terror of 1793? Or under the Directory? It is a fact, in any case, that from 1799 onward they were entirely abolished. An entire century of political struggles would be needed before they could be recovered, one by one, so that they could be passed down to us.

The celebrations which accompanied the second centenary of the birth of Napoleon Bonaparte must not make us forget that his accession and reign resulted in the abolition of all the freedoms gained, in unprecedented administrative centralization, and in police influence even more smothering than under the monarchy—dictatorship of the Bourbons.

It was after this brutal regression that the Reformers began the long and difficult political fight to recover the rights of man. Universal suffrage in France dates no further back than 1848: therefore, half a century was needed to see it once more. The other freedoms did not come until much later still: the Press Law dates from 1881; that on communal freedoms from 1884, like that on trade-union freedom; freedom of association has existed only since 1901; primary education became compulsory only in 1882; and free education at lycées only in 1927.

There were two possible attitudes to take toward the authoritarian regimes which followed the death of the Revolution: one could come to terms with them; or else stand up for oneself by differing from them radically. The politics of this period thus saw the unfolding of the conflict between the opportunists and the first radicals.

The word itself came from England. The English Left was experiencing the same antagonism between the opportunists and intransigents. The intransigents had called themselves Radicals.

The word *radical* appeared in France for the first time in the mouth of a Royalist publication. The Duke de Berry had just been assassinated. The *Gazette de France,* close to the future Charles X, wrote: "The axe of the English Radicals is the same as that of the French Jacobins. On this axe is written: Rights of Man. It is the theory of the Rights of Man which everywhere imperils vested interests, inequalities of condition, hereditary or individual superiorities, and property. It is this theory which threatens the forms under which the nations live in peace."

How many times were these same phrases to be repeated, word for word, again and again?

Radicalism itself appeared shortly after 1830, when people became aware that Louis-Philippe had taken over the July uprising for the benefit of a moneyed bourgeoisie, which reserved fundamental freedoms for itself, and imposed upon the world of labor even harsher conditions than under the Restoration. After 1830, the working day once again began to lengthen, reaching an average of fifteen hours thirty minutes.

47

The first known Radical was a young man, thirty years of age, who, with the money earned by his younger brother, a clerk at the Commercial Exchange (who was later to become a minister of finances of the Republic), was able to pay the poll tax required in order to be able to stand for election to the National Assembly from the Sarthe region.

His name was Étienne Garnier-Pagès. He formulated the two principles which were to guide the Radicals of the first generation:

1. There can be no possible compromise with a government that does not accept the sovereignty of the people and which refuses to guarantee the unrestricted exercise of the freedoms inscribed in the Declaration of the Rights of Man.

2. There is a social question between the classes of society which cannot be glossed over and which is not included in this Declaration. It must also become an objective of the political struggle.

The men of the July uprising did not want to concede any rights at all to the multitude. Nor would they admit there even was a social question. Guizot, the famous Liberal, said: "Society needs to find in its leaders the highest virtues associated with the highest talents. Where and when has it ever been demonstrated that these can be found among the multitude? Where is the proof that the multitude welcomes the views of the most enlightened?"

The demands made by the Radical Garnier-Pagès—that the sovereignty of the people be recognized and the existence of a social question be admitted—seem minor ones to us today. Guizot's position, denying anything at all to the people, seems anachronistic. But this is how the most lucid of their contemporaries—Alexis de Tocqueville—judged the Radicals of the day: "Nearly always living in misery, often coarse, more often extremely presumptuous and profoundly ignorant of political science, the Radical understands only the use of

48

force, and blabbers away with empty words and superficial and general notions. . . . I can understand that an enlightened and sensible man should become a Radical in England. I have never noticed these two qualifications in any French Radical."

Étienne Garnier-Pagès died at forty. His name would be forgotten. But the respect of the propertied classes and their representatives for the "wisdom" of Guizot did not decrease. The Radicals found themselves another leader in the person of Garnier-Pagès' successor as deputy for the Sarthe, Ledru-Rollin, a rich and eloquent thirty-three-year-old lawyer. Because he, too, advocated the sovereignty of the people, and because he reopened the wages question, he was prosecuted in the courts and sentenced.

1848: the twice-restored monarchy expires. The Radicals are on the barricades alongside the workers. Ledru-Rollin enters the government as minister of the interior. He is thus the first Radical to join a government. Louis Blanc, the first of the Radicals to be described as a Socialist, presides over the commission du Luxembourg, in which the social question is for the first time discussed between employers and workers.

In the uncertain atmosphere that results from the fall of the monarchy, with the working-class masses badly organized and the bourgeoisie badly frightened, the Radical-Socialists succeed in reviving some political and social measures: universal suffrage, freedom of the press and of assembly, the abolition of slavery, the reduction of the working day to ten hours. And they submit a draft bill for "free and compulsory primary education."

But the elections are a defeat for all Republicans, Radicals included: the countryside has voted Royalist. The process of reaction once again slips into gear. June: the workers are ferociously crushed. Gradually, everything granted is filched away, except for universal suffrage. The working day, which had been brought down to ten hours, once again lengthens to twelve hours on the average.

It is not enough. The following year, the machinery of the law moves against the Radicals and the Socialists. The "Mountain," their joint parliamentary group comprising fifty-six members, sees its members deprived of their mandates. Ledru-Rollin flees to England. This is the end of the first generation of Radicals. Its fight against the established order of things had lasted twenty years. It was instrumental in raising hope and announcing the future. But it ends with a long night for public freedoms, which is once again called the Empire.

The second generation of Radicals is naturally recruited from among the *Irréductibles* ("unyielding ones") of this Second Empire. When the time comes for the Empire to turn liberal, and when many stern opponents prudently rally to it, a few refuse and lock themselves in what they proudly call an "irreconciliable opposition." Their leader is Léon Gambetta, who presents himself at the 1869 elections and writes above his name: Radical candidate.

This candidate has a program drawn up by his electoral committee. It is called the Belleville program. In it we naturally find the twice-lost freedoms, as well as the principle of the separation of Church and State.

Already we can feel a certain inconsistency between the political questions, which are now becoming familiar, and the so-called social questions. As regards political questions, the Belleville program is radical. But it is extremely moderate in social matters. It simply mentions, as an afterthought, something about "economic reforms which relate to the social problem and whose solution, though subordinate to a political transformation, must be studied and sought for in the name of the principle of justice."

This timidity needs to be analyzed more closely. The Radicals had emerged from an environment in which injustice was deemed to be the consequence of a natural law, that was not to be touched lest the nation lose the road to progress. To pose the "social question" too sharply meant running the risk of cutting oneself off from one's environment and compromising the chances of success.

All men of this period believed, on the other hand, that education could, by itself, give equality of opportunity. This was enough for them. The Belleville program says: "free, compulsory and undenominational primary education, with competitive examinations for elite intelligences, allowing admission to equally free higher education."

Gambetta is elected deputy of Belleville along with thirty other Radicals in 1869, one year before the fall of the Empire in war and defeat. When that happens, the Republic is proclaimed, freedoms are regained, a government with a republican majority comes to power, and Léon Gambetta forms part of it.

Following the elections, the old threat reappears. A peasant vote returns a large majority of Royalists, and even a few Bonapartists. The reaction against the nascent republic, while divided on the dynastic question, brandishes aloft the bogey of Radicalism. What are the Radicals to do?

One half replies: let us be true to ourselves and remain intransigent on our overall program. The other half, obsessed by the precedent of 1848, prefers to join the opportunists— this word did not have a pejorative meaning at the time—in order to install a republic which would be moderate and prudent, but which would be the Republic. The two outstanding Radicals of the period, Léon Gambetta and Jules Ferry, align themselves with the latter half. Did they make the right choice? Can it be said that it is thanks to the concessions made on the Belleville program and the modest "social question" that they succeeded in getting the Royalist peasants to accept the Republic? History does not answer this question. We can reflect on it. The Republic is there.

But this second generation of Radicals found itself truncated by the slide into opportunism. Names such as those of Floquet, Goblet, and Brisson, who remained among the *Irréductibles*, do not stand out like those of Gambetta and Jules Ferry. Two new personalities, who were not among those elected in 1869, then appear to strengthen the quality of the Radicals. One of them is Georges Clemenceau. The name of the "Père-la-Victoire" is too well known to be stressed here. It must nevertheless be pointed out that he left behind him a text whose effects would be lasting and resounding. In a speech made at Marseilles in 1880 he proclaims the link, which will never be erased, between Radicalism and a "progressive tax on income."

Today, economists recognize that the introduction of this tax, far from hindering the prosperity of the most advanced industrial countries, was, on the contrary, indispensable to it. It is to a great extent due to the income tax that industrial societies were able to finance equipment and its infrastructure, thus preparing for further growth and the creative innovation whose root lies in the spread of education.

The other new personality in the world of Radicalism is Léon Bourgeois, less well known but just as fertile. He was the first leader of a Radical government (in 1895 he included in his government's program the introduction of income tax). He conceived, nearly thirty years before Beveridge, the system of social security which now exists nearly everywhere in Europe. He was also the writer who gave its first lasting definition to French Radicalism.

For Léon Bourgeois, societies would gradually lose their religious attachments and their essential objective would no longer be either defense or military conquest. Thus a new solidarity would be needed to link men together. In order that all men should benefit equally, when they come into the world, from the collective inheritance which is the nation, state intervention would have to establish "equality of opportunities," something which exists neither in nature, nor in political society as we know it. The day when this will be considered a duty, this solidarity will constitute a sort of social contract pledging human beings to each other.

At a time when our own advanced industrial societies are drifting blindly, in total nuclear, racial, and monetary disorder, towards a clash of opposing self-interests, this is a concept well worth thinking about.

The third generation of Radicals is faced with a great problem: can there be a party which is simultaneously a party of movement and a party of government? Two Radical leaders went under with the Panama scandal in 1892, Charles Floquet because he had received electoral campaign funds from the swindlers involved; and Georges Clemenceau because his paper had also been subsidized by Cornelius Herz, one of the chief figures in the scandal. The other Radical leaders shirk fighting the government. Their opposition lacks vigor. The main struggle in behalf of the Left is fought by the Socialists. Radicalism is in danger of becoming blurred between the opportunists and the Socialists.

Some young men then undertake to organize reflection and action. They fill the posts of secretaries, or *chefs de cabinet,* to the better-known leaders. These new Radicals decide to explain themselves in a Manifesto. The name chosen is Comité Central d'Action Républicaine (Central Committee of Republican Action). The aim, they write, is to "restore to the Republican (Radical) Party its vitality, its energy and its power for reform."

After much preparation and many discussions, this committee issues an appeal on April 8, 1908. "We wish to submit to you the plan for a Congress for the creation of a party which would be both Radical and Radical-Socialist. It is to be held in Paris towards the end of next May, under the auspices of the citizens Goblet, Brisson and Bourgeois." This constituent congress of the Radical-Socialist Party is held from Friday, June 21, to Sunday, June 23.

Well before the congress was held many observers and intellectuals, such as the Socialist Francis de Pressensé in *L'Aurore,* announced "the death of the Radical Party." There were many, even in the Party, who denied that Radicalism could be simultaneously a party of movement aimed at reforms and a party of administration in the government. But it showed it could, under certain conditions, be both at the same time. It did this over half a century during which the history of the Radical Party became identical, for better and for worse, with the history of France.

To conclude, let us see what lessons emerge from the Radical experience. The first one is that the young founders of the committee from which the Radical Party was born had been right: Radicalism must be simultaneously the party of movement and the party of government, or it is not Radicalism. If it were to limit itself to being a party of movement, which would think of and demand reforms, it would be just one "club" among many others. If it were to restrict itself to being only a government party, in order to improve administration, it would need each time to join the natural majority. (This lesson would shortly appear in similar fashion for the Socialists: Léon Blum would draw it.)

A second lesson is that Radicalism in the French tradition is defined by an essential belief in human reason, in experience governed by rationality. No established vested interest can overawe it, simply because it *is* established. In politics there is no revealed truth; it is always a question of examining and proposing reforms in the light of experience and judgment.

A third and more subtle lesson is a topical one. There have always been vigorous reformers among the Radicals, but they have always been faced by men, in the same party and in every age, who have successfully frightened party militants by giving an apocalyptic description of the disasters which would occur if the reformers were heeded. When the Radical Party heeded the reformers and dared—such as when introducing the income tax, the subject of the darkest forebodings—no calamity ever arrived. When the Radical Party heeded its moderates and did not dare—for instance, in the question of workers' pensions—the reforms came without them—which is to say against them.

The last lesson is that despite some major intuitions, such as those of Clemenceau, the Radical Party was unable to really spell out its mind in economic and social matters. This is the imperative lesson today.

The decline of the Radical Party since the last war did not come about through the wear and tear of power. Power wears out a man, or a team; it does not wear out a party of long duration. On the contrary it renews it. Since 1945, Radicalism proved able to put forward the two politicians who dominate their generation: Pierre Mendès-France and Edgar Faure. Before the advent of Gaullism, no other party was able to provide their equivalent.

Therefore the reason for the decline lies elsewhere. Since the end of the last world war the substance of politics has become, especially for men trained in a legal and literary tradition, nearly entirely economic and social. Our time is an exacting one, especially in the social field, in which Radicalism never really affirmed any conviction and in which, since its thought remained hesitant, its attitude was ambiguous and often weak.

Compulsory and free education, the banning of child labor, the general limitation of the working day, the introduction of a progressive and graduated income tax—these reforms in their day were the crowning glory of the Radicals and the Socialists. They were all, of course, denounced as entirely excessive, utterly irresponsible, and leading irretrievably to the ruin of the economy. Now, it is obvious today that the most prosperous economies are those in which these apparently intolerable reforms have been pushed the furthest. These reforms were not primarily economic in thrust. They were political. But they have played a decisive part in the actual take-off of growth.

The only way of re-creating the revolution today consists in implementing a new, coherent complex of progressive reforms. First of all, we must realize that the reforms we have mentioned have so far been only partially applied. Workers' trade unions do not possess the contractual power required by the operation of a modern economy. The elected representatives of local communities are treated like wards of the state and reduced to the state of courtiers through its centralizing technocracy. There is no progressive income tax in France. Direct taxes are increasingly evaded by the privileged. Neither free education nor the extension of social security benefits can assure to the underprivileged sections of the population equal access to medical care, and even less to knowledge. The sovereignty of economics, after that of the nature of things, still prevents man from moving into a new phase of evolution.

The immense importance of the example given to us by the first generations of Radicals lies in this: much of what was economically absurd in the world of scarcity becomes, in the world of growth, not only possible but necessary for the proper operation of the economy. Henceforth, the structure of authority is going to be less efficient than freedom of initiative in all fields. The maintenance of hereditary hierarchies is a brake to development, whereas the diffusion of responsibilities and measures towards equality are motive forces. Confidence is more fertile than mistrust; transparency and the truth more effective than secrecy and lies, both in business and in the community. In short, technical and economic progress is no longer conceivable without a new degree of morality among men. An entirely new geometry of social relationships has to make its appearance. This will be our task, along with others.

Everything now derives from the economy. Economic growth, linked to the increase of the productivity of labor, constitutes, along with nuclear fission, the most radically new phenomenon of human history. The national income of industrial countries doubles every fifteen to twenty years. As of now, if the working man were content with his ancestors' standard of living, he would need to work only one and a half hours a day. These facts, which date from less than twenty-five years ago, refute Marxist theory in its most essential points. Marx erred concerning the evolution of the standard of living of wage earners, upon which he based his "theory of the revolution." He analyzed the evolution of the relations between bourgeois and proletariat by reference to the only logic of social relations which history, to that time, had given any example: the logic of scarcity. Basing his argument upon this postulate, he reached through rigorous reasoning the conclusion that the capitalist would exploit the worker to the latter's limits of physiological resistance; just as in antiquity the master exploited the slave, and in the Middle Ages the lord exploited the serf. But from the moment when technological process leads to a continuous increase in labor productivity, the main problem for manufacturers became that of widening their outlets. They must seek not only in foreign markets, as Marx predicted, but primarily in the internal market. To do this, the purchasing power of the great mass of workers must be increased, creating a certain convergence of interest between the manufacturer and the wage earner, in which the former benefits from the improvement in the standard of living of the latter. This occurs not because the owner's heart is in the right place, or in order to disprove the Marxist law on pauperization, but because of the mechanisms inherent in economic growth, which Marx and Engels could never have foreseen.

In a society such as ours an absurd equalization of all incomes would represent, for the great bulk of low-wage earners, less of an increase than they are certain to obtain with a few years of expansion. Furthermore, even if it were to be tried, such a levelling-down would, long before it became effective, have created a catastrophic blockage of the whole economic machinery, thus impeding growth severely.

Andrey Sakharov, one of the leading Soviet scientists, a member of the Academy of Sciences of the USSR and three times named "Hero of Labor," writes: "The consumption of the rich, in the United States, for instance, is less than twenty per cent of total consumption, that is to say it is less than the increase in consumption by the mass inside five years. Thus, a revolution which would presumably stop all economic progress for much more than five years would not appear to be advantageous for the workers from the economic point of view. And this without mentioning the blood-bath which inevitably accompanies every revolution. . . . Now, today, forty per cent of the Soviet population—as against twenty-five per cent in the United States—is living in a difficult economic situation; but the five per cent of Russians belonging to the governing classes enjoy privileges similar to those of the American governing classes."

It follows that a rapid and continuous increase of purchasing power is the first requisite of any responsible political action. The primary objective of any new policy must be to maximize the rate of growth, thus increasing the margins of freedom available to the community in order to command its own destiny. The reason why the Radical Party of France is once again aspiring to the responsibilities of power is primarily because it claims to be, from the standpoint of its proposals, capable of running the economy in much better fashion than those in power today.

Marxism is still based on a system of the public ownership of the means of production and the implementation of an imperative national plan. The results of such a system can be seen after half a century of experience in the Soviet Union and a quarter of a century in the People's Democracies.[2] Since it implies a high degree of coercion, the Communist system has shown itself to be particularly suited to ensure a minimum living wage to the entire population—especially in China, where it was most difficult. It also has the merit of diminishing certain inequalities, primarily those suffered by manual workers. Finally, because of its extreme centralization, it has been able to register great success in the fields of military and paramilitary power. But it has proved itself to be increasingly incapable of improving individual standards of living the way the competitive economy has been able to do.

Industrial production is continuing to grow in the countries of the East. But it devours itself and thus is of little benefit to the standard of living. It disappears, so to speak, into the swamp of waste and incoherence which is the system itself. The eminent Czech Communist economist Ota Sik draws this conclusion after twenty years of experience:

[2] We shall see by what reforms these two questions, that of the ownership of the means of production and that of the political ambition of the plan, can now be reconsidered without any violence, or regression.

"This system is incapable of carrying the development of production to the maximum of efficiency, of promoting its quality, permanently encouraging renovation and renewal, and flexibly encouraging structural changes in manufacture. From this derives the deceleration of the population's standard of living." [3]

The purchasing power of the West German worker and the Czechoslovak worker were comparable in 1939 and again in 1945. They are in a very different situation twenty-five years later. Expressed in the number of working hours, their purchasing power can be established today as follows:

To buy a pair of shoes, the German worker has to work for 6 hours, and the Czech worker 17. For a tin of instant coffee, the German has to work for thirty minutes the Czech 4 hours. For an average television set, 130 hours of working time for the German, and 420 hours for the Czech. For a transistor radio, 12 hours of working time for the German, and 120 hours for the Czech.

Ten years ago the ratio of real wages—that is to say actual purchasing power—paid to the Russian, French, Swedish, and American worker respectively was approximately the following: one hundred for the Russian, three hundred for the Frenchman, five hundred for the Swede, and seven hundred for the American. The gap has continued to widen. [4]

Mr. Kosygin is talking through his hat when he says that Communism means rising standards of living. The nation which first launched a space vehicle is incapable of erecting a modern motorworks at a reasonable cost through its own

[3] Ota Sik, *The Truth on the Czechoslovak Economy.*
[4] *Pravda* has just made public some of the revelations made in Mr. Brezhnev's report in Moscow in December 1969 to the plenum of the Central Committee: in several key industrial sectors the rate of growth is slowing down; productivity is growing more slowly than wages; the "bureaucracy" has wasted "a significant amount" of capital investments; food shortages (meat, milk, eggs) persist in "many towns."

efforts; it is forced to ask the Italian firm, Fiat to do it. (Likewise, a modern refrigerator factory, which it has sought from a French concern.) This is more than symbolic.

If the Soviet system today is a powerful brake on the development of Russia (as the most competent economists of the USSR themselves declare, with courage and anxiety, when they are allowed to express themselves), it would be obviously absurd to ask it to be installed, either in whole or in part, in any industrial country of Western Europe. Its implementation would lead automatically to an immediate, general, and profound drop in the standard of living.

The economic failure of the Soviet Union, particularly marked in the agricultural sector, can only worsen relative to Western nations, so long as the system of ideological oppression which is intrinsically linked to it is not transformed from within. Such a system paralyzes, even represses, the individual initiatives which, alone, can satisfy the multifarious demands of the consumers and promote an outpouring of permanent scientific invention, the irreplaceable source of growth.

Consequently, in the field of domestic development techniques, no further hesitation is possible. The choice made by the Radical Party is obviously dictated to it by the aspirations of the wage earners, which constitute a permanent referendum against the Socialist system. This choice is not based upon any doctrinal preference. The market economy, the system of competition, and freedom of initiative, which we intend to use, is in our eyes only valuable as an instrument, because it is more efficient than any other today. While we accept it, we do not accept the capitalistic model of civilization.[5] Our plans and our efforts will be deliberately de-

[5] There is a considerable current of modern American thought which tends to consider that present-day capitalism is a temporary phase which will be subject to profound changes in the future.

signed to break the stranglehold which economic law has on man. The new Radicalism will have one objective: to free man from economic shackles. We are going to spell out the great reforms which are needed, and in the name of this ambition and in order to be in a position to carry out these reforms, we will take as our instrument the free economy with all the power it commands.

As regards business enterprises, production, growth, and standards of living, facts have settled the matter. As regards man, nothing has been settled, and everything remains to be invented. It is the aim of the Radical plan to contribute towards it.

We believe that an improved administration of growth, exemplified by a more rigorous respect of the laws of profitability in the system of production, can and must go hand in hand with a transformation of the relationship between man and the economy, through which man, and man alone, will be protected from the brutality of these laws.

Growth and reform make a whole which can, in less than a generation, found a different universe. This is what used to be called a revolution.

II

The Radical Plan

INTRODUCTION

The Radicals'
Reforms

The work of the first wave of reformers succeeded in transforming certain fundamental aspects of social organization, inherited from the millennia of scarcity, which had reasserted themselves after the ephemeral breakthrough of the Revolution of 1789. It opened the road to economic growth and put an end to the oppressive rule of nature.

The Russian Revolution of 1917, a torch of hope for the workers of the whole world, led to hopes of a second breakthrough, this time a decisive one: control of the productive forces, abolition of social barriers, real equality of opportunity for all human beings, and the reconciliation of man with himself. But like the preceding one, it was quickly snuffed out. In the Communist countries today the situation is not entirely black, but it is darkened by the absence of freedom.

Our generation of reformers knows that the world is too complex and goes too fast for there to be a single answer to everything. But we too must decide to break with the *status quo*, to resume political command, to bring into the world, through the implementation of a new set of realizable political proposals, the things that constituted the hope—formerly a utopia, but now an objective—of the socialist revolution.

Here are the main themes of our reforms for France:

1. *Separation of political power from economic power.* (Chapter Four)

Private wealth and public power are united today in a social nexus through a system of interlocking interests which dates back to Colbert. Their roles are continually being confused but they are in the same hands. By eliminating costly and ruinous state aid, by applying to business firms the rigor of the laws of competition and profitability, considerable resources will be released. These resources will be used to set up an Economic Security Fund for the benefit of all social groups which are the victims of development. In this way, they will accelerate the transformation of our society by investing money in men. If political power remains what it is today—the auxiliary or the guardian of business enterprises—who will look after the interests of individual human beings?

We therefore have to accept the prospect that the declining sectors of the economy will die; but we can refuse unreservedly to accept any diminution of the futures of the human beings who earn their living from them. To do less would be both morally intolerable and of doubtful economic effectiveness, since the anger, or more simply the passivity, of the victims delays all modernization.

We shall thus replace what is pure waste for the community with the most productive possible investment.

2. *Access to social equality.* (Chapter Five)

The major innovation of our generation will be primary education, which will begin in the family and social environment before actual schooling starts. Under the impetus of public power, it can become the instrument which will give the future adult the means of expression, communication, and creation which he will need all his life to be equal and similar to his fellows. Under present conditions the great majority of people are deprived of this possibility.

Subsequent education will then aim at the full development of the individual personality and not just of those skills that are useful in employment. Its objective will not be primarily to adapt man to the requirements dictated by the economy, but to help him to understand the world in which he lives and to stimulate insights into the relationships of things in their entirety. This is the key to personal autonomy. This is also the way to enable such persons to participate in the creation of wealth.

Thus education, instead of consolidating hereditary social structures and careers as it does at present, will attack the roots of inequality and the cultural barriers which, more than anything else, separate the powerful from the lowly from the cradle to the grave.

This means:

(a) Reducing cultural inequalities at their root, before actual schooling even begins. This should start from the age of two, according to the most recent scientific discoveries the beginning of the "golden age of intellect."

(b) Substituting permanent adult education for the far too lengthy period of higher education which is now required. The present system, an unwarranted prolongation of adolescence, breaks the impetus of youth and, throughout life, creates a barrier of university degrees between men.

(c) Instituting a period of civic service (economic, social, and educational) to replace compulsory military service. Students will undertake this during their leisure time, so that they will no longer appear to be parasites, either to themselves (which is often the case today) or to others. These students will be available to reinforce the apparatus of permanent education anywhere—including countries of the Third World should they so wish.

(d) Replacing the system of the Grandes Écoles, the Grands, and competitive entrance examinations in order to widen and extend the recruitment of the country's leading cadres.

3. *The end of hereditary private power.* (Chapter Six)

The control of the capital of business firms—that is to say, the power to run them oneself or to chose the directors —too often remains in the hands of the same families from generation to generation. Private power is thus largely transmitted through inheritance. This is contrary to our philosophy and to the best administration of the instruments of production. Through the abolition of hereditary ownership of the instruments of production we can increase upward mobility in society and accelerate the trend in favor of ability.

We shall achieve this by the reform of death taxes, the complete implementation of which can be accomplished in one generation. Once this is done, the legitimacy of power in the firm will cease to be confused with its ownership. Wage earners will be given the possibility of exercising a direct influence with regard to the choice of directors. This is essential to growth, since even today there can be no effective authority unless it is sustained by the confidence of the staff.

4. *Redistribution of public power.* (Chapter Seven)

The traditional structure of political power, which is at the same time highly centralized and confined within purely national frontiers, no longer allows effective control over the economy. While the private citizen still does not have an effective say in the decisions which determine his future, the government itself has less and less. This is because industrial firms can now establish world-wide empires above national political power; while within the country the dense bureaucratic hierarchy cuts off those in power from local problems and their basic requirements.

Thus, from the smallest unit (commune, village) up to the European Federation, we are going to open new spheres for the exercise of universal suffrage. This elimination of national sovereignty will lead to immense progress for democracy.

FOUR

Separation of Political Power and Economic Power

The separation of political power from economic power can
be accomplished if the community ceases to bear the cost,
both open and concealed, of unproductive undertakings,
whether industrial or agricultural, privately or publicly
owned. The vast and sterile state subsidies will be replaced
by pre-eminently profitable investment in safeguarding and
development of human capital. The resources made available
in this way—a considerable part of the state's budget—will
be used to transform the human conditions of economic de-

velopment. We shall thus offer, as of right, an active—and well-paid—role to the growing mass of workers who, without this public intervention, would be doomed to become parasites or rejects of economic development. We shall thus reintegrate into the community millions of men and women who today are either crushed or by-passed by the process of economic growth.

The continued impetus of a modern economy comes essentially from its capacity to innovate—to invent continually through research less costly processes, more suitable products, more refined responses to diversified needs—and then to integrate them in the process of production. Calculating on the basis of a constant output, any useful innovation reduces the quantity of factors of production put to use: raw materials, investments, and manpower. Thus economic development and the acceleration of technological progress require an increasingly more rapid redistribution of jobs between the different sectors of activity. In order to run the economy effectively, we must, therefore, facilitate professional mobility—not necessarily geographical mobility—that is to say the continued readaptation of the employment structure and individual promotion.

Business lenders, close to the propertied classes and linked to the same interests, accuse the working classes of refusing "the industrial imperative" by opposing the changes it requires. From this comes a permanent situation of misunderstanding and conflict, the forerunner of anarchy. There is nothing more important, if we wish to improve the administration of the national economy, than to end this latent civil war. It is impossible to ask the millions and millions of people left behind by expansion—farm workers, artisans, shopkeepers, marginal or overage workers, unskilled women—today's and tomorrow's victims of this modern scourge of technological unemployment—to accept voluntarily the heavy

71

sacrifice of reconversion, so long as the market laws which are applied to them are not applied first of all to capitalist business undertakings.

Freedom of initiative in economic matters can be supported only on two conditions: the existence of a high degree of competition and full liability for risks involved being accepted by the firm. Competition requires a wide opening out towards the outside world. Some progress along this line has been achieved through the European Economic Community. But the implementation of the Common Market has not even begun as regards those products which are purchased by public or semipublic bodies. And yet these products usually involve advanced techniques which allow particularly big economies of scale. Thus, the supplier of the state remains undeservingly protected to the detriment of the taxpayer and the consumer.

Furthermore, industrial concentration on a national scale such as is now taking place, multiplies quasi monopolies in various sectors. These become so many economic feudal domains, as illustrated by the daily behavior of an employing class which has all too often disregarded risk, and consequently, innovation.

The complete implementation of the free exchange of goods inside the frontiers of the Community is one of the aspects of European unity to which we shall refer later on; it will stimulate development.

These basic conditions—free competition and true risk-taking by the business undertaking—are equally exacting. They presuppose constant vigilance on the part of the public authorities and a real independence from private financial interests.

For several generations now, the law of competition has been violated daily in Paris in the secrecy of ministerial cabinets. Administrative interventionism serves essentially to allow the traditional employing class to invoke liberalism to make its profits and socialization to cushion its losses. Budgetary subsidies and privileged credits, fiscal concessions and arranged transactions, rebates on interest rates, premiums of every kind, parafiscal manipulation, and a thousand different procedures often impenetrable to democratic control take a considerable slice of the national product. They deprive newly established activities or growing businesses—especially small and medium-sized enterprises—of the financial resources needed for their development.

For the most part, this serves only to keep in existence parasitic undertakings whose directors do not need to apply any management techniques. They can practice the more profitable ones of dining in town and playing golf.

The pretext used to justify the existence of this free-for-all is well known. It is done, we are told, to ensure that the bankruptcy of the owner should not cause unemployment for the workers. But it allows the elimination of trade-union militants under cover of small-scale sackings for redundancy, while nearly always keeping top-heavy managerial staffs in existence. In many cases in French industry, the average salary level of management is comparable to that of American businessmen, whereas the wages paid to the workers are three times less than those paid to American workers.[1]

Certain aspects of our public finances are so complex that even well-intentioned persons may be tempted to challenge what has just been stated above. If so, they should read the second program for medium-term economic policy of the EEC, a document prepared by a committee compromising senior officials responsible for the economic policy of the member countries. Drawn up by the Common Market Com-

[1] According to the latest figures provided by taxation returns (those of 1966), 71 per cent of all French wage earners earn less than 15,000 francs *a year*. And 1 per cent of all taxpayers earn over 100,000 francs a year, of whom 0.4 per cent earn over 300,000 francs.

mission in March 1968, it was approved unanimously by the Council of Ministers in December. It says, for instance:

"Public action on structures has not always been satisfactory. Badly informed of the risks involved in changes in this or that field, the administration was led, most often with the laudable aim of preserving workers from the threat of unemployment, to intervene unexpectedly and piecemeal. The common characteristic of these interventions was to protect uncompetitive business undertakings from competition and its penalties. The multiplication of this sort of intervention permitted the survival of often obsolete organizations, techniques, and methods of administration. It has ended by slowing down the adaptation of entire sectors to the requirements of technical progress, thus affecting the growth of global productivity and the increase in the average standard of living that would otherwise have been possible. Furthermore, in many cases, the workers in favor of whom the solicitude of the state was manifested had to content themselves with mediocre earnings, without, for all that, avoiding the possibility of losing their jobs in the long run. Finally, the public resources utilized in these interventions were not available for other more productive purposes."

It is not necessary to be familiar with the arcane style of writing used by international organizations to recognize in this paragraph a piece of criticism with the most far-reaching implications. Especially for France. It is enough to consult the table opposite to see that it is France that is the primary subject of the criticism.

As regards industry and trade, expenditure by public authorities in France (state and local bodies) represents, in terms of the percentage of the Gross National Product, much higher amounts than in the other countries. The contrast with Germany and Italy is particularly striking. The ratio is on the order of 1 to 3.

74

Separation of Political Power and Economic Power

Distribution of public expenditure in 1966
(as a per cent of the GNP)

SECTORS	GERMANY	FRANCE	ITALY	BELGIUM
Transport and Communications	3.0	3.3	2.8	4.9
Industry and Trade	1.1	2.8	0.9	1.1
Agriculture	1.6	1.3	1.6	0.9
Total economic action	5.7	7.4	5.3	6.9
Social interventions	14.2	11.3	14.0	13.3

On the other hand, expenditure on social programs is noticeably lower in France than in the other countries. During the decade 1957–66 the percentage of social expenditures increased everywhere, whereas in France, on the contrary, it has decreased. The sectorial distribution of the state budget in 1969 confirms this particular anomaly of French public finance.

As a percentage of the total of the state's expenditure:

GERMANY

Transport and communications	6.8	
Industry, trade, and crafts	1.6	8.4

ITALY

Transport and communications	7.4	
Industry, trade, and crafts	4.4	11.8

FRANCE

Transport and communications	14.9	
Industry, trade, and crafts	4.9	19.8

75

The funds, officially allocated to industry and trade proper (the crafts' sector being negligible), represent roughly 5 per cent of the French budget, that is to say approximately 8 billion new francs. This sum is far more to the needs of our proposed economic security program.

These figures do not cover, as we can see, expenditure for transport and communications (15 per cent of the French budget against 7 per cent in Germany), nor for large-scale capitalist agriculture. The wastage in those departments, as we shall see, is even more onerous.

Naturally, these figures do not include either the subsidies which cannot be calculated accurately from official documents, nor the fiscal advantages accruing to business undertakings which have ceased all business activity, nor any of the other contractual privileges.

To whom do these public fortunes go? What is their purpose? A recent work *The Industrial Imperative,* whose author, Lionel Stoleru, worked for several years at the Commissariat Général du Plan, presents a detailed analysis of state interventions in the industrial sector. Even though its tendency is capitalistic, this book denounces "an industrial environment run by an imbroglio of competitive policies" and "relief given too much at random," the consequence of a blind frittering-away of public funds.

We can add to this that any decision to give subsidies creates an administrative precedent. Well-founded or not, it has a tendency to be renewed year by year, constituting a sort of entrenched right. Appearing on the subsidy list is the chemical industry alongside the Atomic Energy Commissariat; textiles and leather; shipbuilding; the food industries; not forgetting the coal industry and the steel industry (which enjoys for its own sole benefit a loan from the FDES of 2.7 billion francs over a period of twenty years at a nominal rate of interest); and soon. Who pays the bill? The French people. For whose benefit?

Separation of Political Power and Economic Power

Ill-informed opinion might consider these enormous amounts as investments chosen from among the most productive ones. The truth is different. This entire public effort represents, in the long run, a distorted allocation of resources, very much open to criticism and often ruinous.

The only sector which could usefully be discussed in this connection is the petroleum industry. But the support fund for hydrocarbons is such a "special" Treasury account that neither the Commissariat du Plan, nor the National Assembly have had the right to know what France is paying for its oil policy.

One of the most competent experts, Jean Saint-Geours,[2] concludes: "Most of the economic subsidies written into the state budget are selective, not thought out and a barrier to change. Being allocated to activities in relative decline or placed in difficulties by outside competition, these distortions use up financial, human and physical resources in sectors which are considerably less productive than others."

The reason is clear. And for the same reason, the same confusion of roles, the same lack of common sense the French state is prodigally generous towards industrialists while it is extremely mean with regard to wage earners. The number of operatives in manpower services (worker training) for every million active persons is: 188 in France; 742 in Italy; 898 in Germany!

The Radicals will end this confusion. It is necessary in the public interest to eliminate any capitalist undertaking incapable of developing within the most open competition. The owners of the undertaking, not the state, should bear all the risk and its consequences. That is why, following the example given by the German Social-Democratic Party, which has begun action on these lines, the Radical Party

[2] Former director for economic forecasting at the Ministry of Finance, present Director-General of the Crédit Lyonnais (State Bank), author of several books on French economy.

77

pledges itself to abolish all direct or indirect subsidies of any kind whatever for the operation of capitalist undertakings within five years of its accession to power, except for those designed to improve urban and rural areas or promote research. Nationalized and mixed undertakings will be subject to the same rule of open competition. Their obligations to provide a public service alone will be the subject of specific and contractural remuneration.

As a direct consequence of this same principle, any wage earner, farmer, artisan, or shopkeeper who might lose his livelihood through technological change will be entitled to the fullest possible support from his country. We know how to assure it to them. Material losses inherent in this change will first of all be covered by compensation from the community. The priority development of vocational training institutions for adults and institutions of permanent education will allow those involved to find, in the long run, a better-paying occupation than the one they have lost. As in accident-insurance cases, an indemnity will be paid to cover the moral damage suffered, in order that professional mobility can be secured in the least painful way.

Naturally, the workers will participate through their trade unions in the drawing up of reconversion programs. It is their lives which are at stake; they cannot be the executors of a scenario drawn up without them.

But in the revision of the social security system erected after the war, we have to go much further. Since as of now a person is destined to change jobs and qualifications several times in his lifetime, the risk of reconversion is henceforth the major risk. And we also have to aim to suppress the scandal of misery in the midst of abundance: the misery of the ill-adapted, the inactive pensioners, the workers who cannot be retrained for new jobs.

In this connection, our system of social security has proved

78

very disappointing. Overall, the policy of transferring incomes through social security and the budget—a very heavy burden in France, since over a third of the National Product is absorbed under this heading—hardly does anything to diminish the inequalities arising from the spontaneous distribution of incomes. It barely relieves the unfortunate. The studies made by Chabanol and by Weaver and Jouvenel show that "redistribution is essentially horizontal within each social class; and does not descend from the richest to the most unfortunate.'

This situation contradicts the principle that social security should be synonymous with organized solidarity. Instead contributions are in proportion to income and not progressive; the greater part of them are only applied below a wage ceiling, which is equivalent to exempting higher earnings; and these higher earnings are paid to sections of the population which, in any case, benefit most from the reimbursement of medical and health expenditure. A wide-ranging reform is required.

We shall ensure a vertical redistribution from the richest to the poorest, through the agency of the state which will finance the institution of a *guaranteed minimum wage* by means, especially, of progressively graduated tax deductions from income. It will pay an income, replacing all other forms of financial assistance, to all those whose resources do not exceed a certain threshold and who receive practically nothing from the present system.

Relations between the state, business undertakings, and the workers will thus be transformed in such a way as to allow the most efficient administration of a more human economy. Several consequences will follow. The undergrowth of fiscal privileges designed to serve—and even to remunerate—certain particular interests will disappear, leading to greater clarity within the fiscal system. The restructuring of the budget as defined above will substitute productive expenditure for unproductive expenditure. The continued improvement of the employment structure, which will emerge in the medium term, will be reflected in the productivity gains, which will play a decisive part in the achievement of the conditions of the "magic triangle" (full employment, price stability, external balance). Progress towards realistic prices—not only public but also private—will allow a more rational allocation of resources. A capital market rid of the privileged circuits whch distort it will become more fluid, attracting savings and facilitating the financing of the most efficient undertakings.

Thus we will create the structural conditions for a cumulative process of accelerated growth with price stability. The quality of economic administration will be judged by this criterion.

Thanks to the inflexible application of the principle of separation between political power and economic power, of which the German Social-Democratic Party and the Swedish Socialist Party provide living illustrations, we shall prove that it is possible to combat inflation more vigorously, together with the insidious vices and the whole litany of injustices it drags along with it.

It is most urgent that society should take into account the most dramatic consequences of the law of profitability applied to man himself: those which overhang the "third age," the autumn and the winter of a man's lifetime. Radical policy will show here its determination to overthrow the system of values which economic liberalism unwarrantedly imposes on man.

The facts show that average life expectancy in France was only forty-six years at the beginning of the century, whereas today it is seventy-two years. But the old man, who was formerly the lord of the family, the patriarch, and the subject of a certain social veneration, has now become the reject of our civilization.

In certain civilizations, cruel to the children of the poor and merciless to the weak, those who managed to make their way through life were at least assured of a certain progressive compensation: while an active man's physical faculties would diminish, his moral authority would increase.

In the industrial jungle, where everything tends to depend on profitability, the aged person is increasingly treated as a piece of depreciated material. The sufferings of the old are not only pecuniary but moral. Today, old age is often a nightmare, a jailhouse. "I have seen," writes Simone de Beauvoir, "human beings reduced to total abjection. The huge majority are deposited in dormitories. Through an inexplicable anomaly, the able-bodied are placed on the ground floor, the semi-able-bodied in the first floor, the bedridden in the second floor. The faces of these old women are convulsed with terror and despair. . . ."

In our world, the old are a sort of dross which has to be rejected—and if possible killed. Among those admitted to homes for the aged, 8 per cent die within eight days, 29 per cent in the first weeks, 46 per cent within six months.

Among the characteristic shortcomings of our time, sociology attaches growing importance to the shortage of grandparents. Children need to grow up surrounded by the benevolence and wisdom of their grandparents. But today it is a rare privilege. Cramped housing, destined for speedy deterioration, bans the mingling and continuity of generations. A house, however, is not like ordinary consumer goods. It is a home, the setting of a tradition. Town planning and housing policy must take account of this requisite even though, in the narrow sense, it does not enter into calculations of profitability.

81

Furthermore, retirement falls too often like a guillotine blade on its "beneficiaries." To pass suddenly from full activity to total inactivity is, simultaneously, antibiological and antieconomic. We must therefore establish wide margins of choice, in order that everyone may determine himself the date of cessation of his activity in terms of his own needs. There is nothing to prevent this margin ranging from fifty-five to seventy, provided that pension payments are suitably modified. We shall therefore put an end to the cruel abuses of the struggle against underpaid, overage labor. At present, secondary considerations prevail over the principle. The principle is that aged persons should be allowed, if they so desire, to continue with part-time activity. The secondary considerations are fiscal charges. A better use of the external signs of the wealth tax, an abolition of license fees for older artisans, would get rid of this unnecessarily irritating problem.

A solution must, however, be found for the increasingly acute question of the fate of older workers inside business firms—one of the cruelest effects of economic laws. On this point Japan, whose dynamism is unparalleled in the world, offers an extreme example of the possible. Aged workers are not penalized in the least. Their income increases with their age.

In nations like France, the rush toward the young is partly a fashion and partly because the shortage of educational facilities prevents the older workers from updating their professional qualifications. It is not only savage, but incompatible with the proper use of manpower resources. It is not even compatible with the rules of healthy competition; in the manpower market the most dynamic firms are at a premium. This allows them, even though they pay the same wages, to recruit the most active people and to consign, after depreciation, their worn-out staff to marginal undertakings. Such firms obtain a built-in advantage.

This cumulative phenomenon calls for legislation. Once in power, the Radical Party will propose a rescheduling of the tax on business profits to allow a better balance in the employment of persons over forty. It is not by stupidly copying a foreign social model, but by having the determination and the strength to create one which will affirm our own values that we shall escape the modern forms of oppression.

The first political revolution, that of the Rights of Man, was made by men. The second one, economic liberation, must be very largely the work of women. If the modern world is so harsh in its economic aspects, is it not perhaps because it is nearly exclusively run by men?

The same question lies at the heart of both our social and our private life. Can men achieve a genuine solidarity when they are scarcely aware of the class conflict which is undermining their own homes? While men do battle in public or private affairs, their wives, for the most part, fight only the household dust. At the very time when men begin the decisive rise of their careers, their wives face the change of life, a critical age in every respect. With their children grown up, all too often the only prospect they can see is domestic decline and a gray boredom, barely buoyed by the evening television.

This profound inequality may have served a social purpose at the time when it appeared unseemly for young girls to be educated. It loses all meaning today, when their school and student life is identical with that of boys. The economic waste inherent in feminine underemployment used to be limited. Now it is enormous and even more abnormal, since it results from a small number of unaltered administrative regulations.

The Radical Party is advocating a "policy for life," not just for production, so it is proper that it should place the advancement of those who give birth among its major objectives. Here, as elsewhere, true equality comes from respecting differences, not through uniformity. We cannot assure women a just place in our society by applying impersonal principles such as "equal pay for equal work," the practical results of which remain in any case incomplete. There are activities in which women can excel and in which they are underrepresented. The new Warsaw, built from the ruins of the war, is primarily the work of women architects. It is the only city in Europe which has been so designed, as is obvious when you note that children do not have to cross any streets to go from home to school.

The Radical Party intends to take into consideration the real condition and aspirations of women belonging to different social classes. First of all, those that wish to stay home and bring up their children at the age when they are best equipped to do so—between the ages of twenty and forty—must be allowed to do so. Society should help them to do this by paying them a substantial allowance throughout this period, varying according to particular circumstances.

But if they are to resume working later, they must learn or relearn a trade. Today this is nearly impossible for women aged forty or forty-five. Yet studies made on this subject show that from this age women feel, psychologically, a greater need for professional activity; and that most of them, once they have been allowed their ambition, produce the finest results at work.

Consequently, the tax liability of business undertakings will be modified to induce them to employ a minimum percentage of women aged over forty.

Finally, many women, especially of the working class, start work from the age of sixteen because their family cannot manage without an extra wage. By the age of fifty, they are often exhausted physically, having behind them nearly thirty or forty years of practically uninterrupted work. To them we propose to pay a pension at the age of fifty-five.

Finally, we shall dare to pronounce a word which is never employed in politics. Abstract love of humanity is as terrifying as hatred. But concrete love, felt as an authentic communication, can intervene in the great fight for the liberation of mankind from the vice of economics. Faced with the electronic refinements of the world-wide firm, the civilizing energy which nourishes effort will indeed come from "love, the fertilizing Nile of human labor," as the sociologist Edgar Morin puts it. Let this Nile overflow from private life, let it irrigate social life. What a woman knows how to give to a man, society now asks from its women.

Women, and women alone, transmit life. This biological privilege makes them more suitable in many fields for creation and culture. The examples of Sweden or Israel show that by associating women more completely with the transformation of society, more rapid progress is achieved. Today the food industries and the national education system, in France as in other nations, have relieved women of some of their traditional tasks. A feminine presence is increasingly needed, whether to comment on a television broadcast for children or to arrange a dessert. There is greater need of their reflection, less for their manual labor.

Private or public undertakings are the creative cells of our societies. The feminine presence is needed in them to humanize relations, ensure communication, and finally achieve solidarity.

FIVE

Access to Social Equality

The founders of free and compulsory education believed they had accomplished the revolution: the spread of knowledge would destroy social inequalities and give equal opportunity to all from the beginning. We are very far from this happy situation. In no industrialized country of Europe is the educational system so static as in France. The concept of the public school as the engine of social mobility and movement upwards—which for so long characterized the United States—is not in evidence here, except for a few very lucky and very exceptional students. Americans have their problems of the slum school and the lack of cultural enrichment at home; but France is faced with the great bulk of her students not receiving the lift in life that education can give.

The problem of education, in all its magnitude, is much too complex to be discussed here; but it is typical of all the problems which require getting the entire democratic process to move.

If we are proposing a world freed from the laws of economic "inevitability"; from cheap technological changes which throw men on the scrapheap like a piece of obsolete machinery; from the tyranny of output with its contempt for economically unusable gifts; from the shackles of competition which turns the competitor into a rival or an enemy; and from social predestination which freezes men in castes and transmits class handicaps in a hereditary manner, then this undertaking necessarily implies a searching re-examination of education.

Education must allow men, all men, to dominate change. As change is continuous, it is not limited to a single stage of life but accompanies man throughout his entire existence constantly, opening new doors and new opportunities.

Primary education, as we shall see, can be the instrument that gives the future adult the means of expression, communication, and creation which he will require all his life. Since the educational process is unending, notions of failure and success should be softened. A person who fails at one age or in one undertaking should be able to find other opportunities and still more to come. He should not be relegated to failure all his life. The barbaric distinction between the graduate and the nongraduate, between the *Polytechnicien* and the *Licencié*, an impassable barrier separating destinies forever and partitioning society into watertight enclosures, will be abolished under our program.

Education will aim towards the development of the entire personality, not only of those faculties useful in the battle for employment. Its purpose will no longer be to adapt man to

87

the needs dictated by the economy, but to renew for him the understanding of things in their entirety, which is the key to personal autonomy. Thus he too can participate in the creation of wealth.

Because education will be unending, we will no longer need the indefinite multiplication of the years needed for professional training. The prolongation of study courses amounts to an unwarranted prolongation of adolescence. Young workmen and employees can measure themselves against adults and discover very quickly through their work that they have an outlet for their energies. The student remains isolated from the activities of the adult world. Long after he has attained physical and sexual maturity, he must, like a child, devote his energy to measuring up against other students. He remains in a state of economic and intellectual dependency. This prolonged adolescence breaks the impetus of youth and prevents students from living the life of which they are already capable.

The wall separating "study" from "life" will be demolished. During his long months of leisure the student will no longer appear, to himself and to others, to be a parasite. The needs of the Third World, and of France itself, are acute enough that students are needed to reinforce the apparatus of permanent education. Civic service can allow students to know, understand, and help those who do not share their good fortune. It will replace compulsory military service, which no longer corresponds to any real need and which delays the entry of the young into real life.

Instead of consolidating hereditary social structures and the career opportunities which go with them, education will attack the root of inequality, the cultural barriers which, more than any other, separate the powerful from the lowly from the start of life.

Understood and refashioned in these ways, education cannot (obviously) be kept under the yoke of a centralized bureaucracy. We must introduce freedom of initiative and a certain degree of competition within the public education system and also devise an overall cultural policy in which, for instance, the national television service could find a new *raison d'être* and in which youth and popular education movements will receive financial resources in proportion to the importance of their task. Every job will include a training element. Every man will, in his turn, be both teacher and taught.

We shall formulate two essential proposals to implement and illustrate these themes: attacking cultural inequalities at the base (that is to say well before actual school age) and changing the educational system of the Grandes Écoles to widen the field of recruitment of our country's directing cadres.

Today, the opportunities for French children to receive a higher education (from the ranks of which are recruited the country's directing cadres and managers) are as follows, depending on the father's occupation:

Workers	4.4%
Employees	16.2%
Middle management	35.4%
Senior management	58.7%
Industrialists	71.5%

In spite of a considerable increase in the Education Ministry's budget, the democratization of the University is proceeding terribly slowly. In 1938, 1.6 per cent of the workers' sons were at a university; in 1950 2.3 per cent, in 1960 5.3 per cent, in 1966 9 per cent, whereas we should have reached at least 40 per cent. The majority of graduates of

89

so-called higher education will henceforth be the sons of middle management, not the senior managers as it was very recently. The reason is that a very small number of students succeed in joining the ruling castes through the extraordinary Malthusian system of competitive examinations and the Grandes Écoles. Those who succeed, as a general rule, are the children of wealthy and cultured parents. Thus the social elite remains a fact of heredity. At all educational levels without exception, academic success is directly related to social origin. Recent studies have ascertained this in higher education and prove that the children of the most highly cultured families are directed at the end of third class (when they are either twelve or thirteen) towards the longest study courses and benefit between the sixth and the third from the most intensive teaching.[1]

Ninety-four per cent of the children of senior management, according to the most recent reports, are admitted to the sixth class (at the age of nine or ten) against 45 per cent of workers' children and 32 per cent of rural workers' children.

One might think that the schoolteacher, a son of the people, would make equality reign in the communal school. It is not so. One can read the official report drawn up as part of the preparation of the VIth Plan: "During the elementary course at communal schools, scholastic success continues to improve in direct relation to the social level of their families. For nearly nine children out of ten, their future has been decided at the moment they emerge from the elementary school. Only a minority of ten to fifteen per cent will still be able to change its direction."

One can measure the magnitude of the problem by noting that in Sweden, the most economically and socially advanced

[1] Translator's note: Classes in the French school system run backwards from tenth to first.

European country, "seventy per cent of today's adult population did not go beyond primary school" (report by Mme. Myrdal on "equality" in the 1970s at the Congress of the Swedish Socialist Party).

How does one explain this gap between the objectives of of the early reformers and this situation? Edgar Faure has told the National Assembly: "In highly industrialized countries seventy per cent of all workers should have, or ought to have, a general education comparable to that allowing access to higher education today." Is this another utopia? We believe with Edgar Faure that "it is indeed at school that the redistribution of incomes begins; where in actual fact it takes place."

To understand why, despite the apparently egalitarian mechanism of examinations, free education, and scholarships, the sons of the less privileged are pushed to the back of the line, it is necessary to undertake a complete analysis of the quantitative and especially qualitative shortcomings of our educational system. This shows how the inadequacy of financial assistance prevents low-wage families from prolonging their children's school years; how, within the public schools themselves, the French bourgeoisie maintained separate streams for the proletariat and for the patricians; how first the lycées and then the university have erected the cultural characteristics of the dominant class into criteria for scholastic success—including its failings, such as its contempt for technology and manual labor; and how, finally, a laggard pedagogical system, low levels of staff recruitment, the passion for elimination and for competitive examinations discriminate against the bottom of the class, which corresponds statistically with the bottom of the social scale.

But only by examining two precise examples, that of preschool training and that of competitive examinations and the Grandes Écoles, can we discover the extent to which education remains at the heart of the social question, which economics alone can never solve. In the light of acquired experience and the progress of human sciences, we can see that only education, through the transformation it brings about, will permit the social structure to be really changed.

A decisive struggle is going to be fought in the preschool phase. As far back as we can go towards the origin of a school career, we see the social handicap is a decisive one. Much can be done to reduce it while on the way, but essentially the die is cast before school begins. At the age of six, on the day when he crosses for the first time the threshold of the communal school, which ought to be the cradle of democracy, the workers' son is already less well equipped than the bourgeois' son in aptitude for both reasoning and for communication. He will bear the consequences all his life. There are exceptions, of course, but from the statistical point of view it can be said that six-year-old children are socially predestined and classified.

This is a crucial discovery. At the last UNESCO seminar on Human Sciences on the subject of "the brain and human behavior," it was demonstrated that "the fundamental intellectual bases of the future development of the individual are formed before the age of seven and that the first four years are the most decisive." In a long note to the Ministry of Education, Mme. Laurent-Delchet, supervisor of the Institut Pédagogique National, and Mme. Gratiot-Alphandery, director of the Child Psychology Laboratory at the Sorbonne, draw this conclusion which deserves to be placed on the front portal of the decade we are inaugurating: "The decisive years begin at the age of two. This is the time of mental construction, of representations, of apprenticeship in the language, the time which an American sociologist has rightly named 'the golden age of the intellect.' After this eminently favorable stage has passed, it is too late. The child's scholastic future and no doubt his social future too are in large part decided well before the child enters the reception class."

The English sociologist Bernstein, whose discoveries have been corroborated by German and American research, explains this by stressing the central phenomenon "of the two languages" which coexist in the same community: the elaborated code of the middle and upper classes and the restricted code of the lower classes. The restricted code sums up the experience of a world in which freedom of choice is slight and in which important messages are transmitted more by gestures and actions than by words. It orients the children of the people toward roles of execution, programming them, so to speak, to comply with norms defined by others. It gives them a status involving little initiative. In their future working environment, a simplified system of communication is sufficient for directives to be received and activities to be co-ordinated.

Children of the upper classes, on the other hand, receive an elaborated code, which prepares them to solve problems, to maintain extensive and complex relationships, to grasp overall pictures, and to take the initiative.

They will work on men and on symbols; their less-privileged fellows will work on things.

Apprenticeship to the code, which structures intellectual capacity, occurs in very early childhood, during the first months of dialogue between the child and the mother, when the child begins to register impressions and to express itself. It conditions the subsequent course of the child's existence, starting with his performance at school. Those children who have a restricted code will be more inclined than those with an elaborated code to see the school and its culture as institutions detached from real life. Scholastic failure will have repercussions on the child's professional situation, and consequently on his social status, consumption, leisure, and participation in decision-making.

A society which, thanks to the lightning progress of computers and cybernetics, can free men from material tasks demands, because of this, greater logic, foresight, and mental flexibility so people can adapt themselves to change. In such a society, the handicap of the restricted code becomes ever greater.

The invasion by computers of all human activity, which could be a powerful factor of liberalism and human enrichment, threatens to place the users of the restricted code in a situation comparable to that of the underdeveloped peoples of the present-day world: without any say, without any grasp on events, without power, because the others need them less and less for their own development and prosperity.

In the wake of the research of the great psychologist Piaget, a series of reports has confirmed the crucial role of initial socialization, in the bosom of the family, to the development of the intelligence. Conservatives and moderates deduce from this that a real equalization of opportunities is indeed clearly utopian, because these opportunities are born, or are aborted, within the family—that is to say before the community can do anything about it.

The Radicals reverse the proposition: since the initial environment is the strategic place for human accomplishment, it is where everything must be done. Were political leaders to declare themselves powerless in the face of the annihilation of "the first chance," it could be only because of ignorance, routine, or timidity.

There are many experiments to prove that it is possible to change the conditions of this awakening of the intelligence. In Illinois, education specialists have, inside a year, brought a group of fifteen children from the black ghettos (aged between three and five) up to the level of well-endowed children from families belonging to the urban middle class merely by working with them for two hours a day teaching them language and modern mathematics. In Pittsburgh, Professor Moore has obtained spectacular results by means of the "speaking typewriter," the prototype of one of the richest pedagogical combinations of the future: the combination of the computer and education, tailor-made and adapted to each individual.

Experiments and examples are very numerous, and all conclusive. For the time being, these are only prototypes; but by devoting money to the development of these prototypes—in amounts very much less than what is now used for the conquest of space or for the Concorde or the *force de frappe* —industrial nations could, within a very few years, pass from prototype to mass production.

Roosevelt did not take long to grasp the meaning of the message which Albert Einstein passed on to him in the autumn of 1941. Five years later, the bomb exploded at Los Alamos. How much time will political leaders need to grasp the meaning of the simpler and much more important message handed to them by the pioneers of "the first intelligence"?

We believe that the time has come to invest massively in this very first period of human life, in order to prepare future generations to be more capable than our own. We believe that countries which claim to be advanced can no longer passively accept the destruction of the "first chance," under the pretext that in a liberal society, this is a private matter.

It is not a question of taking children away from their parents; it is a question of showing imagination and helping parents, through large-scale action, to stimulate the awakening of intelligence in their children. Already in several advanced countries, educational experts are advocating the installation in each block of flats of a "children's house" where mothers would leave their babies, from the age of two, for a few hours a week in the hands of teachers specialized in the mental training of very small children. In other countries, networks of domiciliary visitors are being organized. In France, we must achieve the generalization and transformation of prescholastic training. We used to be proud of our nursery schools. But they are inoperative and very inadequate, both in quantity and in quality, compared with our true requirements. From 1964 to 1969, the numbers employed in prescholastic teaching increased by about 30 per cent. This was due to the spontaneous increase in the enrollments of our kindergartens, which proves that demand is high. We have to cope with it through modern pedagogics and more intensively, because, when we look at the figures, we observe that the rate of enrollment at the age of five is close to 100 per cent, as required by law; but it drops to under 80 per cent at the age of four; to 51 per cent at the age of three; to 13 per cent at the age of two. Thus the golden age is already largely wasted.

The problem of the "first chance" is posed especially in the lower classes, where children are deprived of any natural cultural environment because of the harassing nature of their parents' work, the closed world in which they live, the absence of exchanges and any incentive to reading, and the degrading effects of television. It is therefore in the rural and working-class sectors that the task must begin. Once in power, the Radicals will require that the highest possible rates of enrollment in prescholastic establishments be achieved in areas of cultural poverty, in the working-class suburbs of the cities and the least-advanced rural areas.

The awakening and the development of intelligence is still a largely unexplored domain. Considerable investments in research should, in the years to come, lead to breakthroughs of incalculable consequences. France, which in 1968 devoted about 330 million francs to oil research and 77 million francs to research into iron and steel, granted a total of less than 20 million to pedagogical research. The number of professional people assigned to this field is under two hundred! Disorganization, lack of resources and prestige, absence of clear objectives: this sort of research has all the characteristics of underdevelopment.

The National Education Ministry, the leading French enterprise, shows little interest in research, and its bureaucratic centralization in a ministry does not allow it any serious possibility for experimentation. We can thus verify once again that man, having been handed over by the liberal system to the laws of economics, is not only treated like a raw material but often, as is the case here, less well than other raw materials.

The renovation of educational methods depends on research. It requires the democratization and the breaking down of barriers of society. Our objective is not only the sort of equality which consists in placing everyone on the same starting line so that the race should be a fairer one and selection less haphazard. We are aiming at something else. We are trying to lift the lid which weighs on the heads of the poorest. Just as medicine has freed us from infant mortality, previously considered an inevitable scourge, likewise our educational system will have to avoid the mutilation which the present social system automatically inflicts upon the most unfortunate. In this way education will increase most rapidly the intellectual resources of the community and consequently its capacity for the creation of wealth.

Conservatives, in the name of a realistic exploitation of "natural deposits," hold firmly to the rule which reserves the best education for the best pupils. These seem to be, as though by sheer chance, their own sons. This argument is

Malthusian, and we are going to reverse it. It supposes that children, victims either of their parents' lack of culture or of family difficulties of every nature, are unrecoverable. But their recovery is the most profitable of educational investments—if not of all investments. The child of today grows up in a family without a father, and a society without a master. He is helplessly subjected to the temptations, the immediate pleasures, the legendary and captivating universe to which he is led by that parallel school: television. This is a new and even more fearsome phenomenon, since commercial publicity can use its magic freely: the child becomes the target, the prey, and, soon the weapon of marketing experts.

Here, too, there are two sorts of families: those which have the time and the means to give their child an education allowing them to build intelligently on the universe of audio-visual productions, and those which do not. This difference creates a new factor of segregation in the contemporary world. Tomorrow's society is going to depend upon our own understanding of the audio-visual, and especially television. We must change the nature of commercially sponsored programs, if we do not want the next generation to be made up of a majority of infantilized adults.

If the school is to compensate for the deficiencies of the family environment in the face of such pressures, there must be a profound modification of the training and status of schoolteachers.

Because of the blindness of political leaders for over a generation, the "Black Hussars" of social progress tend, in many cases, despite their eminent personal qualities, to form a collective obstacle against the necessary changes in the situation in which they have been placed. The regulations dealing with schoolteachers and professors, conceived essentially to protect them against arbitrary treatment by the administration at the end of the nineteenth century, must be recast to allow state schools to deal successfully with the competition of the system of private education, which is less and less based upon religious differentiation, and more and more on financial discrimination.

We shall, in particular, put an end to the scandal of a society in which a manicurist earns more than a school-teacher, whose social responsibility is enormous. This scandal applies to all public servants. They all bear the same values, and mastery of the economy demands their advancement.

At the other end of our educational system, the system of higher education should be changed, for instance, through autonomy and competition, throughout the entire system, primary, secondary, and tertiary. Our society is still one of castes, very much partitioned. It is composed of closed groups, of bodies within which the reflex of collective defense is stronger than that of competition among individuals, stronger than the interest of the community or even those activities for which an individual is responsible. From this characteristic comes the relative underdevelopment of France.

The caste model can be found at nearly all levels of French society. In the middle—or even the lower—ranges, one can observe a difficulty of communication, on the model of the ruling class. Because it is from the top that the model comes, it is at the top that reform must attack.

The system of the "great corps" in the French government (Finances Inspectorate, Council of State, Mining Engineers Corps) and of the "great schools" (Polytechnique, Normale, ENA, etc.) which feed into them has given France a governing elite of very high quality. It has provided many remarkable personalities. But, hierarchical in its essence, it is perpetuating an administrative and military tradition which no longer corresponds to the requirements of an expanding society. It is preventing the indispensable expansion of the governing group. It is making it very difficult to call upon new talents. It is penalizing new disciplines which do not correspond to the traditional castes. It has created a profound cleavage between the ruling caste and its immediate subordinates, who, since they have no prospect of promotion, are inclined to passivity. It leads quite naturally to castelike behavior among those groups which seek to protect themselves from the higher castes by imitating them. The whole social order is thus frozen into rigidity.

Surveys made in recent years, even by those who have benefited [2] from the "great schools" system, shows that the problem is indeed a problem of system. The two institutions with the greatest responsibility for this state of affairs are the Polytechnique, our main institution for science, and the ENA (École Nationale d'Administration). They are the most prestigious, the most symbolic, and socially the most rigid. The sociologist Michel Crozier makes the following analysis: "Our elite is extremely well selected, the pupils of our great schools are individually very brilliant. Besides, when they go abroad, they are greatly in demand. And yet the institutional ensembles which they form at the 'university-research' level, and the 'business undertaking-administration' level, appear increasingly inferior in international competition. Why is this so? In the same way that it has been admitted that French firms were 'not up to scratch' in the new economic competition, it must be admitted that our small-scale 'great schools,' subdivided as they are, in conflict with another, restrictive, are no longer suitable for true scientific and administrative competition." [3]

---

[2] Including, for the sake of greater clarity, the authors of this book, who, all in all, do not have any personal reasons to complain about it.

[3] Michel Crozier's report on the "ruling groups of Europe" in the face of industrial development was already in the autumn of 1967, over two years ago, the center of our political argument on the American Challenge (chap.

The intellectual tradition of our great schools is a priceless capital asset which must be neither destroyed nor wasted. Furthermore, in the desire for public service, with all that it implies especially by way of material sacrifices, is a form of disinterestedness, which is the virtue of our administration and the strength of its tradition.

Nevertheless, we have to create, at the French or European level, whichever is the most appropriate, much larger centers capable of competing effectively with the greatest and most prestigious foreign institutions. This means creating the equivalent of MIT, Caltech, the Zurich Polytechnic for sciences; of the Harvard Business School or Stanford for business and administrative sciences; and so on. The problem is difficult because a teaching and research institution cannot be built rapidly. We must make use of what exists already and thus develop new institutions.

So we will first merge the whole complex of "great schools" into two or three great universities. From the technical point of view, one regrouping could be effected around the Polytechnique, another one around the Centrale. As regards the administrative sciences, at least two universities will be set up. Mergers at the European level should also be envisaged. These universities would still be medium-sized (from three to five thousand students), but they would nevertheless possess the critical mass necessary to make each of them a first-rate institution.[4]

The second essential characteristic of this new system will be the abolition of the unchangeable hierarchy which, in sciences, puts the Polytechnique in the first rank and makes

20): "The challenge finally boils down to that of changing the profoundly sclerosed systems of the ruling groups. *There is no political power animating development; we are continuing to submit to progress.*"

[4] Note: a graduating class at the Polytechnique today consists of less than three hundred students (as under the First Empire); and at ENA only ninety!

Corps of Mining Engineers the first in this front rank. This method of classification is one of the foundations of the caste system. (An American equivalent would be the requirement of an MIT degree before one could aspire to certain high positions.) There will always be some establishments with a greater reputation than others, but the reputation will not be fixed. It will alter, as in the United States and Germany, in accordance with results and under the spur of competition.

The third characteristic will be the reabsorption of the specialized schools into the new major units and consequently the disappearance of the privileges which appertain to the members of the "great corps" of the state in each branch of the higher administration. The most delicate point for the ruling class to accept—because it is an essential means for the hereditary transmission of power—will be an alternative method of selection to replace that of competitive entry examinations into these universities. There will be no entrance examinations for entry into the new institutions we will create. Selection will be made on the basis of qualifications, marks gained, and schoolteachers' recommendations. Whatever may be the inevitable risks of arbitrary treatment, they are obviously less than the haphazardness and oppression of our present entrance examinations.

In the long run, the ruling class should accept this reform, even though it is perhaps the most difficult one. In any case, it is in its own interests. By agreeing to move out of its antiquated framework in educational matters, to renew its recruitment, and renounce its conservatism, it can, in fact, regain many opportunities which international competition is now causing it to lose.

SIX

The End of Hereditary Private Power

Over half the French people work in industry. Their life depends on the status of the firm. It is natural that this status should be at the center of political debate. So far, this debate has ranged around three systems: capitalism, socialism, and one described as the "third way" between the two classical systems. None of these three is satisfactory, and we have to try to find a way out.

For the advocates of capitalism, it is necessary and enough that the workers should finally understand that they have the same interest in growth as their employers. It is true that in the eyes of economists, and in the medium term—ten years, for instance—the curve of a business firm's profits and that of the wages it pays are nearly parallel. The company which makes the biggest profits in its field pays the best wages. But those who have experience as business directors or as trade-union delegates know that reality is very different from this automatism.

The business director must allocate some profits to investment in order to ensure the expansion of his turnover. He therefore has to resist demands for wage increases. The trade-union representative sees that any improvement in remuneration can only be gained by continuous struggle. He therefore has a clear conviction that wage earners have interests which are quite different from those of their employers.

The system described as socialist, or more accurately as communist, believes this antagonism disappears from the moment that business undertakings become the property of the state, by way of expropriation, or nationalization with compensation. But experience has destroyed these illusions in the countries of Eastern Europe; and in France the nationalized sector suffers from more disputes than the private sector.

In the Soviet Union and all other Communist countries undertakings which are publicly owned work in accordance with the directives of the plan, which determines the aims of production and the level of remuneration. For wage earners, there is thus constant conflict between their desires, their claims, and the responses made by the management. By domesticating their trade unions, the Communist states have merely erased the apparent marks of the contradiction: they have not eliminated it. The wage earner finds himself alone with his own demands in face of the management—

just as he was a century ago in France in face of his capitalist employer before the Radicals and Socialists had asserted the rights of trade unions.

The "third way," a convenient phrase for speechmaking, would like a sort of association, a sharing of power and responsibilities, and a real coadministration to eliminate tensions in labor relations. So far, it has not been possible to implement this in convincing fashion in any industrial country.

In fact, it must be either one thing or the other. Either participation is aimed at associating all the staff in major decisions, which runs afoul of the fact that the staff cannot judge the highly technical and complex problems confronting the management; or participation must be limited to trade-union delegates, few in number, who have received adequate training. But in that case, these delegates, by exercising management power, are cutting themselves off from the base. There is no true participation. Neither system has worked. The Yugoslav system of participation has not allowed sufficient economic efficiency. Coadministration in the German coal fields, on the other hand, has not achieved any significant social changes.

In the passionate confrontation of the three theses in the political arena, their adherents have lost sight of the fact that all three of them are based upon a common assumption: the conviction that it is both possible and desirable to establish constant harmony between all the elements comprising an undertaking. It is this assumption itself which, in the light of modern industrial experience, appears fallacious to us.

The business enterprise, the center of work and creation, illustrates the saying of Heraclitus, repeated by Hegel: "Life is struggle." A permanent contradiction. It is an illusion to believe that its tensions can be erased. This is neither possible nor desirable. Tensions are inherent in progress as in life. The most stimulating tensions are those of the undertaking, those of competition. But to eliminate internal tensions is impossible.

The illusions on this subject in French political life come from peasant traditions. We look on the business enterprise as we used to think about rural property, a landed domain which was an extension of the family. The French word for employer, *patron,* which comes from *père* ("father"), was used before the industrial era to designate the patron saints of the parish. From rural life comes the idea of the workers as people to be protected and taken in charge and finally the conviction that the business enterprise is just one great family in which complete harmony ought to be possible.

In the modern industrial enterprise, the critical distinction is between the three participating forces: wage earners, capital, and management.

In terms of economics, wage earners are suppliers to the enterprise, in the same way as those who supply it with power, raw materials, or equipment. As such, they have simultaneously common and conflicting interests. The enterprise has to be prosperous in order to pay its suppliers properly. But each contract with its suppliers must be the outcome of a real discussion.

A good social policy cannot claim to change the economic nature of the wage-earning class. What it can do, naturally, is to allow those who contribute their labor privileged treatment by contract, comparable to suppliers of material goods.

As for capital, its task is to supply financial resources to the enterprise. It demands simultaneously an income and capital gains on its shares. In an economic system based upon competition and the market, capital must receive its expected returns or the possibility of obtaining new sources of capital, which is necessary for rapid development, is lost. Since the acceleration of economic growth, capital has been changing its nature, though continuing to stamp its mark on the economic system. It is becoming technical. Savings, or small capital funds, tend no longer to risk investment on the stock exchange. Instead they go into trust funds, or investment companies, which are in the hands of the new specialists, the financial analysts. Large funds are beginning to follow the same road. Their owners no longer administer them themselves. They confide this task to third parties who are also financial analysts. The first piece of advice these specialists give is constantly to diversify investment—so much so that the large capital accumulators are now no longer immobilized within the business which brought them into existence. They are increasingly joining small savings in the general mobile capital market. This new conception of financial administration is the salient fact of the sixties and is invigorating the economy. The Radical reform of inheritance law will decisively accelerate this change.

The third factor is management, that is to say, the team managing the enterprise. Insofar as the principles of efficiency require that responsibilities should be decentralized, this team is being constantly broadened. The members of the management team, even though their original appointment may have been made by the holders of capital, are led, because they too are employees, to consider this capital as a mere supplier. What they themselves are seeking for themselves is primarily growth. Capital, on the other hand, puts profits first and growth second as a means of earning profits.

Our policy will therefore take it for granted that there are both common interests and important conflicts of interests between the three elements comprising any business enterprise. Their respective positions have altered considerably. At the beginning, capital alone counted, ruling without any counterweight. Wage earners began to assert themselves at the beginning of the twentieth century with the first political reforms. Their strength varies in different countries, but is almost always very inadequate. Management, which Galbraith has christened "technostructure," dates from a very recent period. Its power is increasing.

It is within this general framework, different from the one presented in classical debates, that the Radical proposals concerning business enterprises have been formulated. These consist of strengthening the trade union, the irreplaceable compensating power for the interest, the defense, and the dignity of the wage earners; opening the way for an alternative to ownership as a source of legitimacy of private authority; and finally accelerating the renewal of the employers' group through the abolition of the principle of heredity.

The starting point for any democratization of economic power is to extend the role of the trade union inside the enterprise itself. Trade unions must be in a position to negotiate, on a basis of equality with the management, everything that affects the condition of the workers, from the small problems of arranging shift timetables—so important in daily life—up to the great questions of reconversion and mergers. But they can be strong enough to negotiate at the top with its partners over major economic and social choices only if they are powerful and alive at the base. It is not the function of political power to put an end to the divisions among trade-union forces in France, but it can help to extricate them from their present condition of poverty and underequipment.

Several formulas have been envisaged. The most effective seems to be that inspired by the German system of help to adult education associations. A compulsory monthly contribution, similar to that financing the social security system, would be paid for each worker. This compulsory contribution would go to the trade-union organization chosen by the contributor. If the latter does not wish to join any of the existing trade unions, his contributions will be handed over to the work's council (*comité d'entreprise*). It goes without saying that before being included in the plans of the government, these proposals will first be submitted to the trade unions themselves.

As regards the way management should be appointed, the solutions of the future are emerging from actual experience. They should not emerge fully armed and helmeted from the imagination of lawgivers, but from the free deliberations of the social partners in the various industrial sectors. Radical legislation will permit and will stimulate innovation and experimentation with all formulas which effectively dissociate ownership from power.

The employer's authority will no longer rest, as it does under capitalist law, upon the mere designation of the owners of capital, or their representatives. It will have to establish itself upon new foundations. Authority, in its traditional form, is less and less suitable. Hierarchy can only work on the basis of free discussion; if it is arbitrarily imposed it is accepted grudgingly. Thus the appointment of a mastering director by the representatives of capital is no longer enough to provide an enterprise with the foundation of legitimacy. The sources of legitimacy are actually much more complex, since they must depend on the confidence of the managerial staff and the asset of all the wage earners.

Instead of being designated by the board of directors, as under capitalist law, the man responsible for the running of the firm could be proposed by the board and appointed by an electoral college comprising three equal parts: the administrators representing the shareholders, the principal management staff, and the elected representatives of the remainder of the workers. In such a college, two votes out of three belong to the employees, and ownership and power clearly cease being confused.

The intervention of the third new power represented by management, on a basis of equality with capitalist and trade-union power, changes the usual terms of the problem and allows innovation without serious risk of injuring the mainsprings of development. The managers, by making, at the bargaining table, a regular examination of the major problems in the firm's life and its development, transform a confrontation into a deliberation. They are employees like the others. But they are also close to the administrators, whose preoccupation with profitworthiness they share. Finally, their knowledge of the undertaking and their competence justify a share for them not only in the daily government, but also in the critical strategic decisions relating to the life of the company.

Our major innovation is obviously the participation of representatives of all the employees, first in the choice of the management, and second in regular deliberation. In those cases where they have applied themselves to an understanding of the constraints of competition, there is no reason why giving a vote to the employees should lead to an undermining of authority.

Several other options, which may differ from this formula in their methods, will be open. We shall thus give to the most audacious, who will also in the long run be the most effective, the right to extricate themselves from the traditions of another age.

The computer, by revolutionizing information systems, is bringing into question the functioning of power, both private and public. It forces the rulers of the state, or of firms, to disengage themselves from day-to-day management, which is increasingly delegated to the "technostructure," and to concentrate on the tasks of promotion, direction, and the creation of teams of innovators; in short, to specialize in the strategy of change and to make the essential decisions. That is their proper responsibility.

We have to be just as exacting about the recruitment and choice of the men who possess private power. Under the law of averages, the heir to a business enterprise is unlikely to be its best pilot. Whether in Germany, Sweden, the United States or Japan—different systems but all endowed with great dynamism—business success is increasingly the work of salaried employees chosen for their competence, outside the circle of hereditary owners of capital. This evolution will be reinforced through the reform of business structures we have outlined. But this is not enough. Another fundamental reform is needed to settle this major question, once and for all.

In a world dedicated to mobility, to give power to those who inherit control over the means of production is a paradox. The principle of competition has always been against mortmains. Each generation needs to challenge all acquired positions, to redistribute wealth, and to renew its leaders. That is why the Radicals consider the abolition of the hereditary transmission of the ownership of the means of production as an objective of major importance, even of primary importance.

Death duties, or estate duties, as we conceive them, will still allow the full right to property as the Jacobins always conceived it: the free personal and family disposal of the fruits of one's labor and savings, whose possession, far from harming society, strengthens its foundations. We shall achieve this by very wide and generous reductions at the bottom end of the tax scale. Once this legitimate relief has been achieved,

the aim will then be to put an end to the hereditary ownership of capitalist power.

The objections which could and will be advanced against
this major reform, either to reject it outright or to delay its
implementation, are all aftereffects dating from the time of
scarcity.

The first is an economic one. Some people still believe, or
pretend to believe, that attacking family-type capitalism risks
injuring economic growth. The observations already made on
the managerial revolution show, on the contrary, that there
is, from the point of view of development, every interest in
abolishing the unearned incomes which this form of inheritance maintains in existence. From this point of view, the
desired change, however revolutionary it may be, should be
implemented without delay.

The second objection, concerning the psychological and
social implications of the problem, is more serious. It consists of pointing out the unpopularity, particularly strong in
France, of any increase in death duties and brandishing the
bogey of a flight of capital to other countries. This objection
must also be rejected.

The sensitiveness of the French on this point is the result of the connivance between political power and economic
power. Whereas the middle classes are affected considerably
by existing death duties and the working classes themselves
also fear them, the very wealthy manage very successfully to
evade them in a thousand ways, more-or-less legal. Once
again, because the little people serve as camouflage for the
big, every reform arouses great hostility.

To reverse this situation, the Radicals wish to point out
that from the moment the decision depends on them, the
great bulk of the population will be entirely and finally released from all fear of death duties. Ordinarily family inheritances, which represent the huge majority, will in fact

be totally exempted, whatever the origin of the inheritance, within a limit which could be set as the total income which a wage earner at the bottom of the scale could earn throughout his life. Even better, we shall implement a policy on inheritances aiming at as wide a diffusion of property ownership as possible.

The formation of a patrimony, especially when it consists, for instance, of a house to which the owner and his family are attached by links of affection, is a normal expression of the personality, a manifestation of individual freedom. It must be free of death duties. With the same objective, the fiscal and civil procedure on inheritances will be reformed so that the son who succeeds his father in agriculture, commerce, or a cottage industry will be guaranteed against the risks of an uneconomic division of the family property.

On the other hand, the hereditary transmission of large fortunes, in whatever form they may be invested (especially where the means of production are involved), will, under this process, be altered once and for all. The heirs will be entitled to a life interest only. Thus, at the end of one generation, hereditary private ownership of the instruments of production will be abolished.

For this purpose there will be a sliding scale in the rate of death duties to be applied against each heir, taking into account such fortune as he may already have acquired. The rate will rise rapidly above the threshold of exception indicated above and will rise very rapidly indeed once an amount is passed corresponding to the cumulative total income of a senior professional man throughout his life.

To calm many fears, we should make clear that the object of this proposal is not fiscal, but economic (fluidity of ownership, capital, and the means of production). It is also moral and social (equality of opportunity).

Apart from that, wealthy persons will be able to avail

themselves in their lifetime of wide opportunities allowing them to assign, either by gift or by legacy, all or part of their property to institutions fulfilling objectives of general interest, naturally without excluding private foundations which it is advantageous to multiply in our country.

The revenue obtained from death duties, which will become a parafiscal source of income, should be allocated by parliament entirely to cultural and health projects, such as improving the condition of those children who are, strictly speaking, the most disadvantaged, the crippled, the handicapped, and those with physical or mental disabilities.

One final objection remains: the flight of capital. Its seriousness demonstrates just how ill-suited the principle of national sovereignty,[1] which today constitutes the main source of fiscal fraud, is to the present stage of economic evolution. Because this situation creates a constraint, there shall be two phases in the implementation of the Radical plan.

During the first stage, France will harmonize her inheritance tax procedure with those of her great industrial partners, especially Germany, Great Britain, and the United States, relying upon them to obtain the signature of the most urgent international conventions. Our country's backwardness in this respect is very great, especially compared with Canada and the United States, and these are not in any case very socialist countries. Furthermore, we shall enlist the influence of the whole of industrial Europe to create a sort of fiscal Interpol, similar to the existing Interpol which deals with criminal matters, as well as to register by computer all large fortunes. The main western governments will support this proposal because they are very worried—especially the United States—by the rapid extension of international

[1] See next chapter.

114

fiscal fraud, as evidenced by the Bank Secrecy Act recently passed by Congress.

This will allow the completion of the second phase and the final ending of hereditary private power. At the end of this phase, a social revolution will have been accomplished which is certainly as important as the abolition of the hereditary monarchy by divine right in political affairs. We shall be able to judge whether the ruling classes deserve to be described as such by observing whether they can understand that, unless they accept this work of justice and efficiency, they will condemn themselves.

Twenty-five years ago, the uncontested inspirer of French Socialism, Léon Blum, declared at the great Congress of his Party held immediately after the war: "I wish that for the first time in our Party history we should speak to the voters about the very idea of Capitalist ownership, that is to say the central notion of any socialism. For my part, what I shall propose to the Party is to attack the essential notion of capitalist ownership, that is to say the notion of indefinite hereditary transmission.

"I do not believe that the question has yet been presented to the voters as being capable of a practical solution, or even as allowing the preparation of a practical solution within a relatively short time.

"It is clear that I am speaking at this moment about capitalist ownership, that is to say the ownership of instruments of production, the operation of which is assured by wage earners. Consequently, I am not including either the agricultural property worked by the peasant, by the owner and his family, or the shop or workshop belonging to and run by the shopkeeper or the artisan and their families. I am at this moment aiming at capitalist ownership as we have always and consistently defined it. I believe that we could envisage

115

that, as regards succession in a direct descending line, hereditary transmission should be limited to a single generation.

"The proceeds of a reform such as the one I envisage must go neither to the current budget, nor to the renovation of the nation's equipment. These receipts are of an entirely different nature and their allocation should have another destination.

"In short, what is the purpose of a reform such as this one, which would still be incomplete since it maintains in existence hereditary transmission for one generation, but which would, by itself, operate a very profound change in our country, which would in any case be very easy to complete later on? Its aim is to establish within each generation equality at the start of the race for all children, whatever their origin or their fortune."

We fully support this statement of Léon Blum, apart from one slight difference, which indicates the magnitude of the reforms possible during the era of growth. For fear of shattering the mainsprings of the economy, Blum did not want to prevent the transmission of fortunes until the second generation. Today one can apply this rule from the first generation. What makes this possible is the confirmed success of many managers who are entirely separate from the ownership of the enterprise they are managing. Since the time when Blum proposed a social reform, which appears rather timid in our eyes, many things have changed. Experience shows us that the life-interest nature of the ownership of the means of production does not harm the vitality of the undertaking. Their present owners will, in any case, continue to enjoy the fruits of their labor and their creation throughout their entire lifetime. Managers who are sure of their creativity—and what other justification can they give for their position in society?—will also accept the annual taxation of

116

their fortune, which already exists in the most advanced countries (Germany, United States, Great Britain, Sweden), just as they have adapted themselves to income tax.

The introduction of an annual tax on building land is particularly necessary. However legitimate it may be for the entrepreneur to benefit from the added value his initiative and his work brings to the community, it is exceedingly abnormal that speculators in real estate should enjoy the same advantage. In one case, the appropriation of profit is the counterpart of a benefit accruing to society. In the other case, the owner of a piece of land undeservedly appropriates a profit resulting exclusively from the initiative and action of others.

The least bureaucratic solution consists in basing this land tax on the value declared by the owners, with publicly owned bodies enjoying a right of pre-emption.

These, therefore, are the principles of our plan to reform private power, its foundations, its exercise, its rights, and its duties in a society based on competition. It will naturally be objected that such reforms overstep the limits of tolerance of the economic system; in particular that they harm savings, the source of investment, and therefore of growth. But new stimulants will arise. Savings will be considerably encouraged, for instance, by a reform of the income tax, which would henceforth only be payable on incomes spent, instead of incomes earned.[2]

At first glance, this appears unjust, because it would mean

[2] This interesting and salutory tax reform has been proposed by Maurice Lauré, one of the great French authorities in the field. In his *Treatise on Fiscal Policy* (*Traité de Politique Fiscale*) he writes: "If we were to substitute the notion 'capacity for enjoyment'—that is to say, income not used for savings, or *spent income*—for income pure and simple, we could adapt the system of income tax to techniques which can be used effectively. This reform so far from being merely tolerable, is actually indispensable for achieving equality between individuals and institutions."

decreased taxes for those classes which save most, that is to say the privileged classes. This objection shows that the proposed mechanism is not well understood and that the present French situation is not well known. During the interwar period, which in France was the period in which income tax was implemented, income derived from capital was taxed at higher rates than income derived from employment. The difference kept increasing until 1948, when the scheduled taxes were abolished and replaced by a proportional tax whose rate was in principle the same, whatever the origin of the income. In fact, even after this reform, the lump sum payment of 5 per cent on wages having been considered equivalent to proportional tax for income from employment (wages, salaries, and pensions), these latter remained relatively favored over income from capital.

But from 1959 onward, the abolition of the proportional tax (it was merged with the graduated and progressive surtax) abolished this discrimination. It is nevertheless an important one, both from the point of view of a conservative conception of equity and from the point of view of our philosophy. The principle of neutrality which inspired this last reform has itself been constantly violated since that time, with the result that tax on earned income in France is not only calculated on a much more rigorous basis than unearned income, but is levied at considerably higher rates for the same amounts.

All the measures taken in this connection in the last ten years have amounted to either a total exemption or a massive reduction of the tax on income from capital. Furthermore, the tax forms for company directors allow some of them astonishing privileges. Tens of thousands adjust, more or less at their own discretion, their declared earnings in terms of their tax position; they can thus systematically merge their own personal expenditures with general company expenses without any check by the shareholders. If we add to this the absence of any general tax on wealth and the lack of any capital-gains tax, it is clear—and it is almost incredible—that France today has the most reactionary taxation system of all the industrialized Western countries.

This is fully corroborated by the table below, which shows the structure of the burden of taxation in the six Common Market countries.

Tax Situation in the Six EEC Countries
(as percentage in 1967)

	INCOME TAX †	WEALTH TAX	TAXES ON CONSUMPTION
FRANCE			
Total	39	3	58
Actual State Taxation	37	3	60
GERMANY			
Total	46	8	46
Actual State Taxation	43	5	52
ITALY			
Total	27	9	64
Actual State Taxation	23	11	66
NETHERLANDS			
Total	57	3	40
Actual State Taxation	56	3	41
BELGIUM			
Total	41	5	54
Actual State Taxation	38	5	57
LUXEMBURG			
Total	53	9	38
Actual State Taxation	50	8	42
OVERALL AVERAGE			
Total	43.9	6.1	50
Actual State Taxation	41.1	5.9	53

† Including the lump sum deduction from wages in France.

How has it been possible to reach such a situation? Very simply: through the pressures which the power of money exerts so naturally over political power.

France has a serious shortage of savings funds available for long-term investment. This situation results from the consequences of prolonged inflation and from the excessive borrowings by the public sector in the financial market. To remedy this state of affairs, taxation incentives have been offered for savings. But they are even less effective since they constitute an admission of weakness by the government as regards its own currency and only encourages the continued flight of capital abroad. The more privileges granted to the propertied classes, the wider are the holes in the financial net. Political power finds, in this situation, one more reason for maintaining and extending the extraordinary high pyramid of incomes which is a characteristic of France. The highest incomes are also the least sensitive to incentives in favor of savings. It is a vicious circle. The history of our financial markets for the past ten years illustrates this fact.

Everything must really start from the base. The incomes pyramid can progressively be brought back to reason only if the public system of guarantees against social risks is in a position to generate a sufficient mass of savings. This is what our proposals are aimed at. If the reform of the social security system induces the wealthy classes to capitalize their fortunes in order to cover part of the risks, the demand for transferable securities from institutional investors will increase considerably.

Furthermore, the implementation of the Lauré system concerning the basis of income tax will not only achieve equality between physical persons and legal entities, it will also create a powerful incentive for taxpayers to declare the amounts of money they have saved each year. Wealth is equal to the net total of all savings previously constituted. Thus through this system of taxation a real register of the fortunes existing in France could be set up. It would constitute the indispensable basic requirement for calculating the annual and general tax on wealth which we shall set up and also for the calculation of death duties payable.

Finally, the reduction of the scale of income tax, inherent in the Lauré system, will be compensated by the extension of the revenue resulting from the integration into taxable income of capital appreciation of every sort.

Insofar as this will improve the negotiable securities market, it will restore confidence to the mass of savers who today find themselves put off by the obscurity of the rules of the game and the lack of accurate information. We shall make our contribution by making it compulsory to supply the name and addresses of all holders of negotiable securities, by controlling all operations on stocks and shares effected by company directors, by compelling all companies to publish their real accounts, checked by trustworthy auditors. This simple measure will permit a rise in value of most French negotiable securities.[3]

The creation, at the national level, of a money market worthy of the name and, at the European level, of the biggest money market in the world, will permit the absorption of the huge volume of shares offered for sale in order to finance the settlement of death duties.

The reform of death duties will also greatly facilitate the carrying-out of these objectives. In fact, the heirs of the great families will have an incentive to take in advance every measure to ensure their shares are kept in good order in case their inheritance is liquidated. Thus, private

[3] With the same general intention, the amounts of tax charged on taxpayers under the heading of Income Tax *will be the subject of a publication,* printed and sold by the state in all bookshops. Citizens belonging to the wealthy classes will have the satisfaction of allowing others to appreciate the size of their contribution to the financing of common needs.

companies would have every incentive to transform themselves into public limited liability companies; the latter would have every interest in getting themselves registered at the stock exchange; the necessity to supply small investors with more extensive and accurate information will become obvious to the main shareholders. A coherent convergence between private interests and the general interest will be established by itself.

Certainly, the reform of death duties will risk injuring the market value of shareholdings in small undertakings, so long as an adequate market for them has not been organized. But in any case, one of the indispensable tasks of economic development consists in creating in France an over-the-counter securities market, similar to the one operating in the United States, where small firms can enjoy the same benefits of public ownership as large.

If, finally, an organism such as the IDI (Industrial Development Institute) becomes by this means the owner of a certain volume of stocks and shares (as is the case in Italy), we do not see that any harm could result from the point of view of general economic effectiveness.

These are some examples of the measures which will accompany and permit our reforms. In a world in motion, equilibrium can only be obtained by movement. Those who claim they can keep the economy vigorous by maintaining the *status quo* are condemning us, as well as themselves. The evolution of mentalities and techniques every day wears out a little more yesterday's cadres. Knowledge calls for reforming audacity, which, in its turn, will accelerate development. Everything lies in that process.

SEVEN

Redistribution of Public Power

The "wall of money" which the reformers of preceding generations met so often is a thousand times stronger today than it was, just as the economy is, compared to the individual citizen. This domination now takes the form of complex overpowerful and omnipresent organizations. Faced with this situation, the crucial task for political action is not to define in advance a complete and fully defined doctrine, but to install, at all levels of political life, democratic organizations capable of operating with the same complexity and diversification as the economy itself.

What does this mean in concrete terms? First and foremost, a new social contract between all citizens, one whose main outlines we have sketched out. Secondly, a whole range of other political actions aimed at lightening the burdens which weigh us down.

We are well aware of the congestion and overcrowding in the streets, the schools, the roads, the telephones, and hospital wards. But we impotently watch while these conditions continually worsen and more subtle, and often more pernicious, problems are created for the future.

One of them concerns the personal relationship between individuals. During the time of scarcity, men were imprisoned inside a rigid hierarchy, but, in compensation, they were part of a web of communities forming an emotional universe. The extended family; the village and the town district with their exchanges; the trade which brought people together—all of these served this purpose. The industrial society extracted us from the hell of scarcity, but it also banished this world of affection. Nothing has so far replaced it. That is why man finds himself alone and anguished in the midst of the "lonely crowd."

In all fields it will be necessary to make the distinction between the positive and the negative aspects of evolution; this is the political task that has to be fulfilled. We can well imagine which questions are going to come first. They are here already, assailing those who have to make decisions. Toward what priorities do we intend to direct the genius of our savants and our technicians? Will it be, once again, toward works of power and prestige? What share shall we assign to the human sciences? The urban areas which will be built up between now and the end of the century represent about twice those inhabited today: are we going to build towns for motorcars, or for people? What type of culture must the education system provide? Toward what sort of housing do we intend to move: the skyscraper block or the individual family dwelling? What price are we prepared to pay for pure air? Is the progress of supersonic transport more urgent than the replacement of internal combustion engines by electric motors? What space do we intend to reserve to physical life within the space and time in which our existence unfolds? How do we want our children to fill their Sundays, and their Saturdays, and their Thursdays? These are some of the real questions involved in politics. On each of them, the big companies have their own precise and profitworthy ideas; that is their business. Their strategy is being implemented. But what of ours?

It is obvious, for instance, that aircraft manufacturers are going to do everything to achieve supersonic transport. They activate their pressure groups, the professional journals, the technicians' associations, and even the trade unions. Then, a thousand-voiced rumor subsequently assures us that it is urgent to allow those who, in the world of princes of industry, are referred to as the "jet set"—the thirty thousand people at most who go round the world several times each month—to make the Paris–New York round trip in one day. But how about everyone else? Has a survey ever been made which measures the general interest of the project in terms of the overall cost?

Oil-tanker vessels are becoming gigantic, because the oil companies wish to economize on freight charges. A 500,000-ton ship costs much less to build and turn round than ten 50,000-ton ships. But then, publicly owned organizations dispute among themselves, at the cost of billions, for new harbor facilities investments—at Rotterdam, Le Havre, Antwerp, Fos, and Genoa—in order to have the capacity and the honor of welcoming these monsters. This gigantic debatable expenditure for the transformation of harbors is unavoidably charged to the taxpayers of each country. Who has ever worked out the actual cost of these operations to the general interest?

These same oil companies earn their living out of the sale

of petrol for the millions of internal combustion engines that power our motor vehicles. Motor manufacturers are now investing in new production lines, already planned today for 1980, designed to mass produce indefinite versions of these same engines. Such powerful groups are obviously in no rush to speed the arrival of the electric motor, even though it alone is the answer to the problem of air pollution. Why should they seek a discovery which would ruin their plans?

No one can counter any longer the strategy of the large firms, dictated by their own interests, with their own body of doctrine, general and intangible, fashioned a century before the problems facing our industrial society. But this does not mean we must submit to the far-from-enlightened despotism which is the mark of this technocracy. As the level of economic development rises, society acquires an increasingly greater freedom of choice to apply to changing conditions. Continual adjustments are necessary. As society becomes more complex and more mobile, the foundations of rational action are reversed. In the simple, hierarchical societies of scarcity, efficiency required respect for orders sent down from above. Now it rests upon surging innovation, and solutions are possible only with the concurrence of those who will have to implement them. Revolution, in this field, therefore consists of a radical change of legitimacy.

In the last resort, the judge can no longer be a "guardianship authority" of any sort. It must be the entire people, simultaneously called upon to rid itself of archaic behavior and to embody the profound hierarchy of values it carries within itself.

Such are the principles. Within this framework there will be an optimal localization of centers of decision. It is here that the reality of democratic power in its various forms will have to be established.

126

At the highest level, it will manifestly be the entire world. The idea of a world government is one of the oldest utopias of men. But we have already seen the profound response and unexpected respect which Pope John XXIII aroused with his encyclical "Pacem in Terris": "The peoples will have to submit to an international juridical order disposing of adequate executive power." Not many years later, the specialists are expressing the same urgency. The American biophysicist John Radar Platt writes: "The present generation is the hinge of History. . . . We are perhaps living in the period of the most rapid changes in the evolution of the human species. The nuclear world has become too dangerous for us to content ourselves with anything else but Utopia." And the German prophet Robert Junk: "There is no hope except in the gradual withering away of States."

The primary reason for this is easily understood. Five countries in the world today possess the atom bomb. One can admit, as an assumption, that the levelheadedness of five governments is enough to preserve peace. This may be why we still survive. What will happen when there are ten, then fifteen, and then twenty? And if a country possessing the bomb falls into the hands of a dictator, and this dictator finds himself in desperate straits? At best, only fifteen years remain to us to answer these questions of life and death.

But in the economic and financial field immediate reality is taking us by the throat even more. General Motors' turnover is already comparable to the French budget and it is growing twice as fast.[1] The French cybernetics expert Robert Lattès writes: "According to present trends, about sixty companies can dominate the entire world. . . . Even before 1985, they will achieve together an annual business turnover

[1] As for the net profits realized by General Motors, they exceed the net profits of the whole of French industry.

of 1,000,000 million dollars. The leaders of this spearhead will each have an annual business turnover greater than the French budget. Therefore, in terms of financial power, several of these giants will be more important than France. Nearly fifty of these companies will be of American origin and all of them, willy-nilly, having been forced to join in the game of the great wide open economic spaces, will have extended their area of operations to the entire Earth."

So long as they remained inside the framework of their country of origin these great business enterprises were, partly at least, contained by the authority of the state. What will happen when they become transnational, as are nearly a hundred firms today, of which four-fifths are American?

They do more or less what they like. The German Director-General of the Siemens concern M. Gerd Tache speaks very frankly: "We are at home everywhere." When Unilever, the Anglo-Dutch company whose business turnover is $5½ billion, and Nestlé, the Swiss food concern whose turnover is $2 billion, decide to go into partnership to exploit a part of the market in a particular European country, what is there to prevent them from becoming a monopoly and destroying all competition, apart from a certain inbuilt business morality? What is there to prevent IBM, which manufactures 70 per cent of all computers in the world, from seizing the entire Italian market for itself by playing fast and loose for a while with the laws of competition? Nothing except the restraint of its executives.

We cannot leave it to the moral sense of business leaders to preserve the market economy from monopolies. We must demand, as a matter or urgency, the creation of antitrust legislation on a world scale with a court of justice to implement it, analogous to what has existed at the Hague for over half a century to settle legal disputes between countries. This court of justice should be given executive power as well. Similar measures must be implemented, as we have already seen, to prevent tax evasion.

Meanwhile, there is the unprecedented problem of the Eurodollar. As we know, banks create money by issuing loans for a higher amount than the liquid cash they keep as a security reserve. In all countries, the issuing authority (in France the Bank of France, in the United States the Treasury) controls this creation of national currency.

Yet today, the international department of the great private banks can create "international currency" without being subject to the direct control of any public authority. About 90 per cent of the deposits received by this banking sector are in dollars, since the dollar plays a preponderant part in international transactions. These are the Euro-dollars. The prefix *Euro* indicates the region of the main locations (the great European business centers and London especially) in which the middlemen operate, but there is no controlling authority at all.

The problem posed by the Eurodollars is a brand-new one. It is not primarily the possibility of ruin of the banks which receive and accept them: the dominant part played in the system by the subsidiaries of the great American banks guarantees cautious and prudent management. The danger lies in the asymmetry of attitudes adopted towards this problem by the American authorities on the one hand and the European countries on the other.

The American government does not worry about it. Quite the contrary, the amount of funds involved is largely determined by the United States' economic and monetary policy, and the Eurodollars, because they are actual genuine dollars, can, in accordance with certain accounting conventions, help the American balance of payments. Added to the enormous privileges already attached to the American dollar in its capacity as a reserve currency, the Eurodollar system makes the United States the only country in the world which enjoys today the freedom to pursue its economic policy regardless of its balance of trade.[2]

The situation of the European countries is the opposite. First of all, the mass of liquid funds involved (35 to 40 billion dollars in 1969) considerably exceeds the overall monetary mass of any single country of Continental Europe. It represents, for example, about twenty times the foreign exchange reserves of the Bank of France. Certainly the amount of gold in the vaults of the Bank of France has recently decreased considerably. But in order to understand the real seriousness of the situation, it must be realized that even in Germany, the leading world power in monetary reserves, the authorities were forced to exhaust all the liquid foreign currency reserves in order to meet the withdrawals of Eurodollars that followed the revaluation of the Deutsche mark in 1969. The Federal Republic was even forced to sell five hundred tons of gold to the Federal Reserve Bank to finance these withdrawals.

Thus, even a minor shift of the mass of Eurodollars from one country to another can lead to terrible disturbances in balances of payments. The system runs the risk of either creating inflation or forcing certain countries to take restrictive measures resulting in bankruptcy, unemployment, and so on. So is another blind and uncontrolled power set loose.

In our time, the mobility of short-term capital has greatly increased. It results not only from improved techniques but also from a requirement of good management: company treasurers whose field of action is international have the

[2] The anomaly of this situation cannot be overestimated. If there are any countries which ought, in equity, to be allowed the possibility of being freed from external constraint, these would be primarily the underdeveloped countries.

obligation to invest their liquid funds most profitably. It is part of their normal duties to borrow money in a country whose currency is due for a revaluation, as has been done on such a wide scale in the last few years. It is not a question of morality, but a right.

Thus, the great banks, with their power to create money with the Eurodollar system, coupled with the part played by the great American companies in the countries of Europe and the generalized acceptance of the dollar, have become direct competitors of the money-creating powers in the national systems. In these conditions, "national monetary sovereignty" becomes a meaningless expression.

Faced with this situation (which has proved very expensive, especially for France), what can the European countries do? If they continue to act in isolation their only recourse is exchange control, which, in the long run, constitutes a sure technique for underdevelopment.

There are only two solutions: either to persist in the policy of monetary independence, leading to the economic decline of each country, or to organize ourselves, as European countries, into a union matching the size of the United States.

A united Europe would represent the leading world power in the field of international trade and monetary reserves. It alone could counterbalance the United States and establish a world monetary organization capable of mastering the new forms of monetary creation which govern the whole of economic and social life.

In the long run, then, the problem of world organization overhangs our survival. In the meantime, it overhangs our prosperity and our capacity for decision. For France, the question is whether we are to continue to be a part of what Françoise Giroud [3] has so accurately described as "The Club of the Murderers." Biafra–Nigeria. What really took place

[3] Journalist, editor-in-chief of *Express* magazine.

131

there? The classic game played by chancelleries. The industrial nations acquired markets for their arms industry through the massacre of the black tribes. And when, today, the Nigerian government forbids foreign observers to go and see what remains of the Ibo people and what has been done to them, no so-called civilized country objects. Let the Ibos keep on dying then, provided that respect is maintained for the reactionary principle of nonintervention, and for the absurd and bloody taboo of national sovereignty.

Israel and the Arab countries. The same system applies. If France did not sell warplanes to Libya, others would do it, says the government (not succeeding very well in hiding its shame). But what is France doing in order to change this situation for the better? And yet, with all the evidence we have, the only solution is that suggested by Françoise Giroud: "the export of modern weapons should, by joint international agreement, be completely and entirely banned, from all producing countries to all consuming countries."

Who is there to enforce respect for an agreement that tampers with so many merchant and national interests linked to each other so closely? No one, so long as there is no universal law, nor the means for enforcing respect for it.

"The first arms-producing country submitting such a proposal will perhaps make itself very unpopular with some governments. But it will be the only one of whom it will be known by the peoples of the entire world that it refuses to belong any longer to the club of the murderers." This is Françoise Giroud's conclusion. It is also that of the Radicals. We should hope this country to be France.

Is it tomorrow that these actions, so urgently and vitally necessary, will be organized on a world scale? The skeptics smile. But we well know that the day after tomorrow, a young generation will arise which knows no frontiers. Perhaps they will be able to create a first world government to master the unacceptable. Let us hope there is still time.

Meanwhile, we must pass through the indispensable stage of political organization of the continents. This work lies within immediate reach of our generation. To answer the immediate imperative, our countries must first endeavor to operate seriously within Europe: a considerable framework in which they can act without any serious difficulty.

We thus return to the theme of the United States of Europe. Not quite as it was presented by three generations of fervent devotees, as a sort of ideal to be defended by the finest. But rather as the indispensable framework for concrete action which has to be undertaken as soon as possible. In order to create antitrust legislation, to bring Eurodollars under control,[4] to limit tax evasion, to take a census of fortunes, to stop Luxemburg from continuing to be the site for the head office of so many holding companies which wish financial haven, to stop Switzerland from benefiting simultaneously from all the advantages of being located in Europe and all the profits accruing from its systematic encouragement of fraud, and so on.

The Radical Party, for the reasons we have just sketched out, will join with all other European parties which share, in essentials, its ideal and its philosophy. It will draw up a contract of association and action. Let us not underestimate this possibility: draftbills submitted simultaneously, on the same day, by the reform-minded parties of all the countries that comprise Europe can have a considerable impact.

Once in power, the Radical Party will undertake with its partners, who are already engaged in it, the foundation of the United States of Europe. We will have to catch up on

[4] M. Raymond Barré, the French vice-president of the EEC Commission, declared (at last!) on January 15, 1970: "Today, the European currency is in fact the dollar; the American Federal system is in fact the lender of last resort of the European central banks; there is no European capital market, but a Eurodollar market; European industrial structures are increasingly tending to be fashioned by the investments of American firms."

the terrible delay which occurred during the sixties. Its foundation will be popular sovereignty. There will be a European Parliament based on democratic legitimacy, with a senate elected by universal suffrage, in accordance with arrangements fixed by each state.

The United States of Europe will have a multinational collegiate executive, elected by direct universal suffrage. The rules for this will be decided by the Council of Ministers on the basis of a proposal submitted by the commission. The task of the elected federal executive will be to draw up a draft federal constitution within one year. This fundamental text will lay down a strictly limited list of the powers properly and jointly pertaining to the Federation of the United States of Europe. These powers will cover the European currency, defense, foreign policy, and an economic strategy of balanced regional development.

The Radicals will propose that the draft of the European Federal Constitution define the general principles of a long-term plan of aid for the Third World. This aid will be dispensed within the general framework of regional organizations grouping the recipient states.

This draft constitution should be approved by the European Parliament. Time presses. Transitional periods were necessary for the Common Market, since the relaxation of barriers disturbs an economy before it strengthens it. But in the case of a political union which the people want, which will be the source of freedom and the means—the only means—of realizing a great ambition, a transitional period does not make sense.

Paul Valéry [5] could never have imagined just how the history of France, in the sixties especially, would prove him right when he wrote: "Politics is the art of preventing people from busying themselves with what concerns them." At the

[5] (1871–1945). Poet, philosopher.

same time that the national state was becoming increasingly impotent in the face of the world-wide problems of the economy, the national civil servant was caught progressively in a system which made him a real hierarchical superior to both the citizens and their elected representatives. Unlike the United States, where state and local government have strong responsibilities over important areas, in nations like France all is directed by the central bureaucrat from the central ministry.

This must be changed. The region and the commune are, after Europe itself, the indispensable levels for political action as we conceive it.

Whether the number of regions in France should be ten or fifteen is a debatable and secondary question. The main thing is that they should be conceived on a European scale and solidly established around the poles of attraction which are beginning to form a spider web of relationships around regional metropolitan areas. They should be fully fledged territorial authorities. This has a precise meaning: those who will form part of the Regional Assembly will have to be elected by direct universal suffrage. Could they possibly have less legitimacy than county councilors, when they will have more powers? These regional assemblies will have a president, elected by their members and responsible to them. The regional prefect will play the double role of head of the regional state services and representative of the national government in the region.

Circumstances have made the limits of the urban commune those of the agglomeration itself. Similarly rural communes can no longer be kept inside a framework which is often only the current version of the parish of the Middle Ages. It is up to them to regroup themselves in accordance with their wishes, the state helping them or deputizing for them.

In any case, the rural mayor and his town-hall secretary

must be honored and preserved. These modern tribunes of the people, amiable mediators with extremely wide-ranging knowledge, are the human face of the administration. Better still, they ought to have opposite numbers in every district of the utterly soulless cities. Many young men leaving American universities today prefer to work in social action rather than embrace far more remunerative careers. They go into the neighborhoods of the cities. France has a long way to go before reaching that state, but it is one of the roads to a better future.

Traffic jams, pollution, noise, lack of open space in the cities; monotony, isolation, boredom in the rural areas: these are the key problems with which local authorities are concerned. They are also primarily responsible for making available facilities for relaxation and celebration, for sport and entertainment. All this is pre-eminently the business of politics. For the words *urbanism* and *politics* have the same root; one comes from the Latin *urbs* and the other from the Greek *polis*. Both signify *city*, and both are vital to our future.

But this reform implies that freedom of initiative and real responsibility be given to elected representatives at the regional and communal level, and they should be freed from niggling paper work and the need to obtain prior authorization from Paris. This innovation must necessarily be translated into financial terms.

The reform of local finances is a familiar problem. The present tiresome inaction must be ended, and principles must be defined for the communes and the department, which will also apply to the regions. Local authorities must be in a position to equip themselves with their own technical services. Without these they are doomed to impotence and irresponsibility. If the mayor, the Chairman of the County Council, and tomorrow the regional president always have to seek approval, as they have to do today, for their roads and public thoroughfares from a chief engineer appointed by the *Ponts et Chaussées* department in Paris, whose appointment and career depend entirely upon the state, it is illusory to hope that these local authorities can become really autonomous. Therefore, an end will be made of the quasi-monopoly of technical services by the nation in the planning and implementation of regional investments. Some of the officials belonging to these services could be assigned to the various regions, departments, and communes and placed under the exclusive hierarchical authority of their responsible elected representatives.

This break with the lazy practices of the past will not take place without difficulty. Every change implies an apprenticeship. Failures will occur. Universal suffrage is there to sanction them. It is only thus that new elites will emerge who can assert themselves by means of the choices they make.

At the same time, the tax system will be radically modified. Local authorities will have wide freedom of choice concerning optional taxes and dues. As for compulsory taxes, it is important that those which affect the pockets of taxpayers most closely—especially the income tax payable by individual taxpayers—should be employed to finance expenditures which are immediately apparent and clearly identifiable. This means that the income tax must become a regional and communal tax.

The citizens are not blind. If they are Parisians, they see the contrast between the refined luxury of the head offices of the great companies and the shabbiness of the hospitals or Social Security departments. If they live on the shores of the Mediterranean, they see the contrast between residences described as "secondary" and the miserable condition of municipal services. We should cease to stand by while this progressive pauperization of public services, the mark of liberal societies, proceeds. This state of affairs can only be remedied with money, and this money can be levied only if the taxpayer can connect what he is paying with what he can see.

Finally, the very conception of financial relations between the state and local authorities must be reversed. The undergrowth of piecemeal state subventions, which shackle elected representatives and poison civic life, must be swept away. A single global subvention will be paid by the state to all the local authorities in a single region, its amount to be determined largely in terms of the policy of territorial development. It will be set sufficiently high to counter the natural tendency toward increased inequalities of development between various regions of the nation.

Local authorities must simultaneously have freedom to borrow, subject to the common law of the market, and freedom to manage their own financial affairs. Accounting control, previously exercised by national Treasury services in advance should be replaced by a subsequent audit, allowing the deliberative assemblies and their citizens to gauge without delay the technical quality and the suitability of their management.

Paris deserves separate mention. It is the only city in Europe without a mayor. Its administration is directed by two prefects, placed under the direct hierarchical authority of the minister of the interior. This is its punishment for the faults committed by the 1871 Commune. After a hundred years, Paris is surely entitled to an amnesty.

The liberation of Paris will take place at the same time as the creation of the regions and the lifting of controls over the communes. It is important that Parisians should become citizens enjoying full rights, but it is also important to put an end to the scandalous and ruinous tradition according to which provincials are considered as second-class Frenchmen. This is the underlying reason for our geographically unbalanced growth. From the moment that a high proportion of creative intelligent people abandon the regions and the smaller cities in favor of Paris, further homogeneous growth is no longer possible.

We must remember Benjamin Constant's [6] advice: "Multiply, keep on multiplying the clusters which unite men. Personify the country at every point as in so many different mirrors." By modifying the country's political architecture, by introducing the regions into it, a first step will be taken. By appointing to regional and municipal technical services a considerable number of state officials, a second will be taken. With increased powers and increased means, the municipalities will be able to make their cities and towns more attractive.

But the vitality of local authorities is not enough to counter the natural aggressiveness of industrial firms and bureaucratic centralization. The citizenry must find new reasons for living by participating in various sorts of voluntary organizations. Spontaneous organizations, born out of free initiative, whether they are concerned with art, sport, mutual aid, the progress of ideas will increasingly become the schools of personal autonomy and seedbeds of active citizens. Their multiple networks of influence will establish the bases of a functional democracy, inserted into the daily realities of life, and also the system of values, outside economics, of the new society.

Despite the progress of automation and management, there will remain many small and routine tasks to be performed both in factory and office. The more the effort of adaptation alters the personality, the more necessary it is that

[6] (1767–1830). Romantic writer, politician, promoter of liberal ideas in France; author of *Adolphe*.

there be places in which the man in the street can educate himself to live in the community, taking an active part in full freedom and according to his own desire.

The evoluton of social habits is beginning to go in this direction. Pierre Mendès-France has noted: "In this country, which is claimed to be indifferent and depoliticized, we can see groups multiplying, especially in those places where new forces are being awakened and are at grips with acute problems: this is the case in the rural world.[7] We observe that everywhere where people are grouped together, or where a collective need is felt, where the public has to be informed of the existence of a problem in order to intervene with the authorities, everywhere where there is a need for collective decisions, an appetite for working in common is manifested, within appropriate organisms operating democratically."

We shall have to try to help these new political groups to widen the range of their action and take an active part in all sorts of associations—not only in trade unions. The Radical Party will offer the representatives of these groupings the possibility of more active participation in its own life and the progressive elaboration of its program of government.

Such, therefore, is our conception of the distribution of power and of the people's sovereignty. We see a whole series of new decision centers, ranging from Europe down to the village and the district level. This choice of different levels for political decision is in itself a revolution, since for centuries the nation-state alone has been the setting for important decisions.

Another began to emerge with the formation of a united Europe. But Gaullist philosophy blocked progress on this

[7] We shall return to this subject, because Mendès-France here touches on a very important notion: the civic example given by a growing number of farmers.

point more than any other. When a conviction such as Gaullism is held so deeply, it is necessary to halt a moment and to listen to its poetical translation. André Malraux writes: "The twentieth century has been the era of national wars. When we look at Africa, it is just a collection of nations. When we look at Asia, where the national idea had probably never existed, it is now the land of the Indian nation and the Chinese nation. When we think of the last upholder of what was the International, that is to say Stalin, we remember that, looking at the same snow falling which buried the Teutonic Knights and the Grande Armée, the Georgian Stalin said: 'I have made Russia.' The world in which we live is a world of nations and any political thought which fails in the first place to present the world as it is, is a vain thought."

This brilliant fresco covers everything except the facts which concern us. It is not by accident that the examples quoted by Malraux are of countries which were under-developed at the beginning of this century and, for the most part, still are. As regards the developed countries, the apogee of the doctrine of the national state was the nineteenth century. It led to the absurd and final catastrophe of the World War of 1914. The Second World War was no longer that of the nations. The victorious army, which won the final decision in the air, at sea, and then on land, was a federation of the armies of different nations, under an integrated command that had come from another continent.

Certainly, the nation has not lost its reasons for existence. A warm reality in people's hearts, a collective link of solidarity and memories, it can be preserved and improved, but within the federal settings which are the way of the future. What must be abolished is the absurd and total concentration of all public power at the level of the state.

Nationalism has corroded the fundamental and noble idea

141

of public service. The government official, because he has to preserve the so-called sovereign rights of the state and work within a national framework while denying the world-wide and all-pervasive empire of economics, is forced to operate in the setting of a quasi-military hierarchy, giving orders to people without receiving any either from them or from their representatives.

By diffusing public power everywhere it can really operate, we shall change this state of affairs, just as we shall change it for private power. In the name of one and the same idea: to wrest power, everywhere we can, from fate or inevitability, to hand it to men themselves. Whatever the setting, the nature, the place of power, once again as always, it is a question of handing to the citizens of tomorrow a real grasp over the direction, the trends, and the decisions on which their lives depend.

What will they do with it? That is up to them. But if we can eliminate the aftereffects of scarcity and loosen the stranglehold of economics, they will be in a far better position to use it with nobility.

III

The Future of
the French People

EIGHT

Does a Model Exist?

To get some indication of the results of the programs we are suggesting, it would be helpful if we could find, somewhere in the world, a society which embodies, wholly or in part, the system of values and the ambitions which we have defined. But when we examine those countries which are famous for the efficiency of their management or the quality of their political life—the ones that would be the natural models—we find we can draw different lessons from different societies.

Let us begin with economic growth. Consider Japan: in expansion, it leads the world. How did it achieve this? A very bulky book would be needed to explain how, and it is an extremely fascinating story.[1]

[1] There are two very instructive and recent books: those of Professor Hubert Brochier and M. Robert Guillain.

While running the risk of oversimplifying, it can be said that Japan proves that the best way of developing a country is not necessarily to force it to imitate the American model. This is a lesson France should not ignore. The aim of *The American Challenge* was to underline it. Our leaders repeat persistently that in France, geographical mobility of manpower must be increased at all costs; the state must be excluded as far as possible from economic life; business enterprises must be self-financed where possible, enabling them to reach a level comparable to the Americans'; executives of mature years must be replaced at top speed by young dogs of thirty; and most significant, our controllers must be of one mind and agree "to rehabilitate the law of profit," as they say.

The distinctive features of the Japanese economy are quite the reverse: the practically absolute immobility of manpower; the coexistence of the most powerful political planning system in the world with the weakest rates of self-financing; a system of gerontocracy, with advancement by seniority; and an attitude towards incomes and money which means that wages and salaries paid depend almost exclusively on degrees possessed and age reached. All these characteristics are directly linked to a specific conception of the Japanese socio-cultural heritage.

Does this not give cause for reflection? Technological progress extends the margin of choice available to each society when the moment comes that it must decide to remain itself. Many ambitions will be based on this verified truth. For the rest, Japan is the antimodel incarnate.

Where there is no social security system, the fear of illness and old age means that personal savings are absolutely compulsory; there is only a slight degree of social mobility; a plutocracy rules which sacrifices community amenities to mercantile values, creating generalized traffic jams, turning road travel into an obstacle course, allowing concrete to massacre the most delicate landscapes, transforming a formerly splendid sea into a sewer.

The opposite example, without a doubt, is that of Sweden. It is a model country in so many respects that it is difficult, in our age, to conceive any policy of economic and social progress without reference to the experience of Swedish Socialism. It is not only a fashion to do so. It is an object lesson which grows continually richer in what it has to teach.

Sweden has managed the best synthesis between techniques of the competitive economy and the objectives of Socialism. Its social system is the subject of universal admiration. Yet, the country is still not satisfied, and the Social-Democratic Party in power continually seeks for new weapons for the great fight against the sufferings of mankind.[2]

Finally, its conduct in international affairs is dictated by morality. Its prime minister is a man who, while minister of education, dared to lead a street demonstration against the war in Vietnam, resulting in the recall of the United States Ambassador and a crisis in relations with America. During the historic debate in the Council of Europe at the end of 1969 to condemn the fascist regime in Greece, France tried everything it could to get this regime absolved; it was Sweden which fought, alongside Federal Germany, for man and his rights in Greece.

But even Sweden cannot be our model. One of the characteristics of Swedish society is that it tends to identify a good policy with happiness. Insufficient attention is paid to the ambiguity of the human condition. The abolition of suffering, even moral suffering, will not be enough to make man happy. This might explain certain individual difficulties

[2] The previously quoted report by Mme. Myrdal on "equality in the 1970s," which lies at the limits of utopia, was unanimously adopted by the Swedish Socialist Party congress in winter 1969.

of a psychological nature which are noticeable in Sweden.

The most advanced members of the new Social-Democratic team in Sweden consider that the concentration of Swedish business undertakings within a property-ownership system that has remained essentially of a family type, will pose serious problems in the future, if only from the economic point of view.

Finally, Sweden is Sweden. It has a population of only eight million people, who are pure Nordics. It cannot be a model for a France, which, within the United States of Europe, will tomorrow conceive its role as being based upon a powerful integrated and planet-sized community.

As for the great world power, the United States, we can finally understand the lessons it offers. Some are of tremendous importance for the rest of the world—not only in the exploitation of scientific power, but even more in the intelligent organization of teamwork, which is a key to the future. But so long as she herself does not form an integral part of Europe, France will continue to perceive in the United States only a deformed caricature. And this Europe itself cannot be, must not be, another America.

In addition, there are the unique problems of American civilization: poverty amidst affluence; crime and violence amidst opulence; the tragedy of indifference to racial injustice; and the resumption of the cycle of inflation and unemployment. Finally, relationships between individual persons are pervaded by the view that economic inferiority is a reflection of the inferiority of the individual person himself.

But America is a world in itself, a composite, enormous federation, in a perpetual dialectic. In America hope has always been rewarded. On the shores of the Pacific and on the banks of the Potomac, young people are demanding that these conditions be ended and that society offer them a morality for our time. Continually destroying and recreating the best and the worst, America today is, at the frontiers of the human adventure, the great and mysterious matrix of the future. As it begins more searchingly to question itself, it is becoming what Europe has always been: a continent of history under interrogation. For all these reasons, while we must study America, it cannot give us our model.

Germany, however, is a different picture. It is perhaps most immediately useful for the French people to cross the Rhine, rather than the oceans. We have not had the good fortune that Germany and Japan have had; all Germany's history prepared her to triumph, after the military battle was over, in the industrial struggle. It would be a bad dream to wish, like some do, to recreate another Ruhr, either around Paris, or in Lorraine, or in Flanders. But it is no coincidence that Germany is the country most often quoted as a reference in the pages of this book. For Germany has succeeded admirably in freeing herself from her history. This is what France must do as well. What Germany has done as regards Bismarck and Hitler, we should do to Napoleon, his heirs, successors, and admirers. Germany is also the example of regional vitality contributing to the movement of the nation's unity in the direction of the future. There is no one center in Germany. Munich, Frankfurt, Dusseldorf, Hamburg, Berlin—all are hubs of independent wheels of activity. Her municipal experience, her Socialism—described as social-democratic—would itself deserve a visit from French ideologues. The strength of her currency merely synthetizes the quality of her social organization, which is symbolized by the power of the workers' trade union, the DGB. Experiments in comanagement are a significant form of participation. They constitute seeds which will ripen.

All in all, the closest example, most fertile in both immediate lessons and concrete hopes, for what we wish to do, is Germany. Especially today, when she has handed power over entirely to the party which is not that of the businessmen.

Thus, France can find much to borrow from Germany and Sweden; some from the United States; and even from Japan. And that is not all. In economics, sociology, and politics, as in biology, progress often proceeds in accordance with a dialectic of assimilation and differentiation. There are other patterns in other lands. The lessons of Great Britain under a Labor government are valuable: the strategy of an exceptionally difficult industrial recovery, based on a permanent dialogue with the workers; selectivity in profit-worthy undertakings; the excellent organization of the money market; and the multiplicity of information. Fair play and humor in public life, characteristics in which France has hardly shined. An art of life, a sporting feeling in all things. British democracy, as we see it morning and evening on television networks, is one from which we can learn much.

Italy gives us two examples that are worth their weight in gold. It is possible today to make a profitable industry out of the raw materials of art and beauty. The other: great risks are incurred by continuing to follow the traditional law which says that factories should not be moved to where the men are, but that men should move to where the factories are. Beware of the deportation of workers from poor regions to the great industrial centers, as Fiat has swept up to Turin the men of Calabria. It is better to put factories in the sun, than uproot men in the cold.

Benelux, and especially Holland—a great nation, a living experience of the Radical hope. Holland shows us that the maximum opening to the outside world is not only compatible with the maintenance of individual cultural characteristics, but is the prime condition for their enrichment.

150

We cannot omit even the USSR as a source of examples. The material and moral revaluation of manual labor; the progress of the equality of the sexes in salaried work.

Since both politics and civilization are involved, we can borrow much, provided that it improves the heritage of the past while offering opportunities for the future. But after this trip around the world we must conclude that a strict model does not exist. No country, no society has yet achieved what we propose the French people accomplish. In order that France should have her future, French people must invent it.

Not the Radical Party alone! The time of the prophets has passed. We are only one component part of our own plan. It is only in the debating chambers of national, regional, local, and operative democracy with many groups and parties participating, that this enormous task will be worked out.

Therefore our proposal here, to end this work, is not to present a completed plan, nor even a completely sketched-out proposal; but, after having set forth general lines, to give a few concrete illustrations of the actions we shall undertake.

France is entering a new phase of her history. Two factors dominate, because of their importance and the constraints they place on political action: the size of the country and its social texture. France's population will increase at a relatively rapid rate during the next few years. Normally, this should lead to a national leap forward. But France is a country of medium size, characterized by a marked decline over the past half-century. While we cannot claim a big power role, in the classical meaning of the word, other forms of leadership and influence are open to us. But let us accept the elementary truth of the limitations of our size. Let us be willing, in accordance with a new political drive, to convert some of our most deeply rooted and fallacious ideas, mentalities, and aspirations.

In the modern world, size compels. France finds herself in about the same situation as that of a medium-sized undertaking on a market it cannot dominate. To succeed, it must specialize in the fields in which it excels. To grow is to choose.

The impetus and growth of innovation in our time leads to an exponential diversification of products, manufacturing processes, and marketing. This diversification implies that each economic unit should specialize further and that, in parallel, its market outlets should be widened.[3]

To be the first, to be the best, in any field whatever, is the central problem of any undertaking that wishes to prosper. It is also the central problem of all countries that do not have the size of the United States.

But the more a state is centralized, the more its reflexes slow; and the greater tendency it has to spend its main efforts imitating what has already been achieved by others. Thus the structure of the French budget for scientific research singularly resembles that of the American budget, through no other reason than the inertia of our rulers and their error of vision.

Developing our economy by way of specialization, turning away from the wastages of false power, discovering new forms of grandeur, no longer based upon the principle of a strength we no longer possess, these are, for us French, the imperatives resulting from the country's size in the industrial world.

Out of all the middle-sized great countries, no other requires so great an effort to achieve a conversion of this sort

[3] The nation, in this perspective of the strategy of growth, will be considered a constellation of economic units.

because of the social structure it has. Everything in our social structure recalls that we used to be, primarily, a great military power, not lacking in aggressiveness.[4] Our economy was conceived on the model of an arsenal, a poor structure for free international exchanges.

Many natural factors explain this essential character. The diversity of resources, climates, and ethnic groups found gathered together on the half-million square kilometers of the French hexagon, the richness of the soil meant that up to our generation France was self-sufficient. From this derived a social structure dominated by the archetypes—strongly hierarchized—of a patriarchal peasantry and a military organization. They explain the power of the administration and the degree of centralization which, we have to remember, are unparalleled among advanced democracies. In accordance with the same logic, the French bourgeoisie, instead of turning toward industrial and commercial activities based entirely and resolutely upon freedom of initiative, has never stopped living in a state of concubinage with the state, convenient but ruinous. These traits underlie the social structure of the country. It proved very capable of making its way within the constraints of the world of scarcity; but through this very fact, it is much less at ease in the world of growth.

France is having great difficulty extricating herself from her traditional protectionism. A century ago, French prices were at least 50 per cent higher than those of Great Britain, and our coal cost four times more than English coal. But France was self-sufficient: she was content to produce what she needed then in very small runs. Yet the lower tariffs

[4] The handbooks written by Ernest Lavisse, or Malet and Isaac, do not always make it clear. But the more one travels abroad, especially Europe, the better one understands that the spirit of conquest and a certain pretension are the two least-appreciated features of the images of France.

of the Commercial Treaty, signed in 1860 by Michel Chevalier,[5] initiated a wave of astonishing prosperity for the French economy. This lasted until the Third Republic—with the complicity, it must be said, of the Radicals—capitulated to the lobbies which the Second Empire had cowed. As early as 1892, Méline [6] raised customs barriers and triggered off a process of decline and economic sclerosis, from which the country only began to recover when the Treaty of Rome, creating the Common Market, was signed fifteen years ago.

Another major aftereffect of self-sufficiency is the extent of inequalities in France. From a qualitative point of view. this is illustrated by our political and administrative life. Jean-François Revel [7] notes perspicaciously: "The French politician does not consider himself to be the representative of his people but its owner. . . . Our politicians have seen in the people only an instrument on which to play their narcissistic melody. This state of mind can be found at the level of many senior public officials as well. Neither the former, nor the latter, regard themselves as employees of the people, which they are in fact, but as hierarchical superiors of the consumer or the citizen."

As for the business undertaking, it is not by accident that Fayol,[8] the classic authority on the subject, conceived it on the model of the Napoleonic army, with a sort of emperor at the top of a pyramid, both as regards the lines of authority and the distribution of incomes. It is true that our business undertakings do not make sufficient profits. But, in very real measure, this is due to the fact that senior management

[5] Who is so accurately described by Pierre Drouin in his book *The Europe of the Common Market* as "the Jean Monnet of the time."
[6] Jules Méline (1838–1925). Minister of agriculture during the Third Republic.
[7] Author, philosopher.
[8] Henri Fayol (1841–1925). Engineer, administrator, advocate of industry by hierarchy and authority.

(which is often overstaffed) is paid too much and the wage-earners at the bottom of the pyramid too little.

The hourly wage paid to the French worker is today one-third less than that paid to the German worker. Yet the net per capita national income in Germany is only 4 per cent higher than in France. The difference is considerable. How does it arise? The recent studies, undertaken by Pierre Uri [9] in particular, show much higher average incomes in France for the privileged classes. After twenty-five years of Christian-Democrat administration, Federal Germany, in terms of the distribution of the national income, proves to be much closer to the USSR than to France, where material inequalities continue to worsen.

The last essential trait of France is its great number of individual, national, and regional characteristics. What vitality our ancient provinces must have shown to allow regional feeling to resist so many centuries of centralizing laminating! "The foundations of French culture transform themselves hardly at all, and they will continue to give expression to the values which we associate intimately to the French nation," notes Laurence Wylie, the finest American observer of French society, with great satisfaction.

We must keep this situation in mind in our strategy of French development. The economist Kindelberger specifies precisely what is meant: "It has long since been remarked that demand for mass-produced articles has always been a low one in France, owing to the taste of the French for elegance in their consumer products. Individual work is preferred to the products of the machine. This very lively interest in the work produced by the individual artisan has allowed, for instance, Sèvres porcelain and the Gobelin tapestries to perpetuate their existence into our own day. For less durable products, the Parisian clothing industry already

[9] Economist, counselor at Atlantic Institute.

offers the classic example. . . . There is there an element of economic specificity which, certainly, poses some serious problems in the epoch of industrial concentration, but which, if we know how to handle it, can also be exploited with great profit."

The drama of recent times is that these vital national characteristics have been treated with contempt because of lack of understanding of modern relationships between economics and politics. Were we not on the eve of the opportunity to remedy this state of affairs, this could make us weep with rage.

NINE

Changing Course!

General de Gaulle brought dignity of conduct to state affairs and put an end to the demagogic excesses which had characterized a too-long-drawn-out tradition of debased parliamentarism. His role in France will be remembered not just in the hearts of the people but in the strength of the country.

Yet under his influence there was little progress toward the goals we seek. What is stagnant today is less French society itself—though our rulers say and no doubt believe it—than the policy of France, a policy of yesterday with its tenaciously alive remains.

Those who see a sclerotic, archaic, and stagnant France as a sort of natural phenomenon—almost quasi-geological— are wrong. We see the image of a people which is disenchanted because it has been for too long misunderstood and

157

misgoverned. Military policy is designed less to defend the country than to allow it to keep up its ranking. Our economic policy has concentrated research not on the best methods of development, but on those which were thought to be the noblest: those which would prove more striking to the imagination. The major purpose of energy policy was, according to a minister himself, to be "patriotic." Monetary policy was not designed for stability or solvency, but to constitute an arsenal of gold reserves capable of putting the dollar to rout. Out of all this, only ruins remain, about as useful for the growth of our economy as the casemates in the Maginot Line were for our independence. Unless we admit this frankly and clearly, we shall never extricate ourselves from this situation.

The "patriotic" energy policy has resulted in such high prices for electric power in France that one of our most brilliant profitworthy enterprises, Péchiney, can no longer continue to invest in aluminum foundries in France and has instead installed itself in Holland and even the United States.

The monetary war ended with the weakening of the franc, which, compared with the Deutsche mark, lost over 40 per cent of its purchasing power between 1958 and 1969, and with continued exchange control, which in the long run is a serious obstacle to growth.

Let us not even speak of the billions expended on the *force de frappe*, but let us not forget the thousands of high-quality research workers which it wasted.

These policies had as their counterpart a secret obsession with the American model and a subterranean colonization of France by it. This was quite natural, as it constituted the very image of power which was being aspired to. Yet the bulk of the industrial development fostered by the state is a poor copy of the model. Its key sectors have been nuclear energy, the aerospace industry, and electronics. The aban-

donment of the national graphite-gas reactor to foreign reactors is only one sign among many of a general failure, the
consequences of which the government is refusing to draw.
The pretentious Plan Calcul, despite the benevolent and
occult collaboration of American companies, is continuing to
absorb millions in money and some irreplaceable brains with
doubtful results.

This American model, which is doggedly being foisted on
the French on a small scale, can only be, and is, a mere
caricature. The law of profit, of which there is so much
high talk, continues to ignore the requirements of competition, as shown by the creation of quasi-monopolies on a
national scale under the pretext of industrial concentration.
As we have seen, the state budget and many different administrative procedures gravely handicap the effectiveness
of competition by arbitrarily conferring advantages on certain undertakings. The prevailing view about the geographical mobility of the workers continues to be inspired by the
example given by the United States, but not by France,
disregarding the fact that the United States is much more
culturally homogeneous and has much more of a tradition of
movement from place to place; but also disregarding the fact
that many Americans strongly resist having to leave their
communities in search of employment. The examination of
the policies toward farmers, shopkeepers, and artisans also
allows us to measure the seriousness of the deviation.

To map out some markers on the way to a real development, we shall first indicate the two major economic direc-
tions for France; and then the particular action to be taken
concerning socio-professional groups.

The two essential lines of development concern housing
and land development (urban and rural) on the one hand;
and the motive forces of development on the other. The

two are closely linked. The housing problem, one of the most serious in France, was not brought about by blind fate. It was created through a series of wrong policies. If the price of cars had remained fixed by the state for more than a generation, there would be a shortage of motorcars similar to our shortage of dwellings. Rents were brought under control in 1917. They have still not been entirely decontrolled. Some people have been given rights as sitting tenants—which means a lot of other people remain homeless. And these, of course, belong to the poorest sections of the population. There is an object lesson in this for the city of New York.

Because of the shortage of housing, the state decided to build some itself. It was, as Alfred Sauvy [1] demonstrates, the best way to make the shortage permanent: "At the end of this process, the INSEE (National Statistics Institute) showed that there are more people with large incomes in the HLMs [2] (state-built blocks of rented flats) than in the country as a whole. On the other hand, in the HLMs, there are about three times fewer low-income families than in the country as a whole. Even taking rural families into account. The disproportion remains overwhelming. If the well-off families paid a normal rent, the low-income families could be given a home free of charge! Faced with such a situation, the watchword is silence. . . . Nothing becomes more easily antisocial than a law with good social intentions, if very careful attention is not paid to its implementation. Here, the dispute is no longer over money, but over who profits from the law." [3]

The situation is even more serious from the point of view of amenities. Most housing now being built injures the French landscape and depresses those living in it, even though one of our dearest traits, considering the national

[1] Sociologist, well-known specialist on demography.
[2] *Habitation à loyer modéré:* Low-rent housing.
[3] Alfred Sauvy, *Le Socialisme en liberté.*

temperament, is precisely the sacred character which many of us attribute to the family home. Ours is not a country where a man sells his house in the same way he sells a car. That is one value we must preserve.

In this policy area, we need to make a completely new start. All rents in the private sector must be decontrolled. Local authorities must be given the means to carry out their duty, which consists, in the first place, of creating a sufficient supply of building land at reasonable prices and establishing the infrastructure necessary for urbanization. Our reform of the system of taxation is in line with the first objective; the creation of the regions and the transformation of communal structures corresponds to the second.

France, along with Italy, is the only country of Western Europe in which the housing problem remains serious. This is due in large measure to the fact that France is the only country of Western Europe in which local authorities are not capable of action.

To complete the solution to this problem, we need to ensure the liberalization of capital markets, encourage the development of the savings movement, and implement the principle of economic security. All these measures are included in the Radical plan, as well as the institution of a guaranteed additional allocation of resources. By taking such action, it will be possible, over a period of fifteen years, to solve the housing problem in France, as it has been solved in Germany.

At the same time the excessive number of those seeking secondary residences (greater in France than in the United States) should be enabled to find in their main place of residence the conveniences they expect from the other. This policy requires an entirely different approach to town planning and land development, both urban and rural. We have been officially forewarned. The group of experts appointed

161

by the government and sitting with the Commissariat du Plan has written in its report that by 1985 France will be characterized by "twice the crowds, three times the bottlenecks and traffic jams, four times bigger suburbs."

It is absurd to resign ourselves to this in the name of blind economic fate. It is necessary and possible to institute a new right, a political right: the right to beauty. Beauty is a vital necessity: it is as indispensable a raw material to a really human life as are water and fire.

France has a marvelous tradition of popular enjoyment of serious culture. Taxi drivers wait in line outside the exhibits of the Grand Palais. At the time of the Popular Front, the museums were kept open until late in the evenings after the factories had closed, and the workers crowded into them. The French go by the thousands to visit Versailles and feel better there than in the bleak industrial city, because Versailles is a fine conception, each part in harmony with the whole. On the other hand, we are struck by the hideousness of the interminable peripheral areas around most of our great cities. We are shocked because there is nothing in them that accords with a wider prospect.

The new conditions of economic development and the release from natural constraints which follow it mean that government can localize its activities, more or less where it likes. Let those who want to live either in the mountains, or at the seaside, or in the sun be allowed to do so. In the long term, if the appropriate economic measures are taken, this can be realized.[4]

The uncontrolled growth of cities, spreading like oil slicks,

[4] Why, on the contrary, does the Master Plan for the Paris region provide that the population of greater Paris should increase from 8,000,000 inhabitants today to 14,000,000 in the year 2000? It seems that the public authorities believe themselves in the presence of a blind fate. Labor policy, on the contrary, has succeeded in steadily reducing the population of London.

is the source of great evils. There must be an entirely new conception of cities, modern, autonomous, and of human dimensions. The optimum would be around 200,000 to 300,000 people, a figure that reconciles the requirements of collective investment with the greatest possibility of satisfying the housing needs. Furthermore, it is less expensive. The reform of local authorities, which we have proposed, can bring about this great change on the face of France as regional vitality replaces centralizing repression.

But the major problem in the development of the French economy is that of its industry. "The French," writes Roger Priouret,[5] do not like their industry." This is true and serious.

The implementation of new policies with regard to town planning and the broader efforts to free mankind from oppressive economic constraints are in line with this purpose. But this is not enough. A new approach must dominate the selection of the main lines of French economic development. Present concepts date back to the period of semiscarcity and reconstruction which followed the War. Rationing and shortages reigned everywhere, owing to bottlenecks in coal, electricity, steel, fertilizer, transport services, and especially the railways. The state thus had a duty to draw up a list of priority development sectors and to obtain, by any means available including tax levies, the financial resources needed to satisfy the most urgent needs. Hence, the implementation of a particularly ambitious budgetary and financial policy and the creation of the national plan.

These techniques were useful, but the habits which were acquired, and the success achieved, persisted for too long.

Two other factors reinforced them. The system of development established was in line with the Colbertian tradition of an administration which never gave up the new powers it

[5] Journalist, specialist on economy and industry.

acquired. Then, a substantial current of ideas favorable to *dirigisme* and nourished by what then appeared to be the miracle of the Soviet economy reinforced administrative prerogatives defining the main orientation of the economy.

Only one thing counted at the time, both in France and in the Soviet Union: increased production. The notion of international competition had hardly any meaning, since the French economy was protected by customs duties, quotas, and exchange control. The consequences of this protectionism were inflation (and the social injustice resulting from it) and a relative weakening of our industrial structures, the consequences of which we are still paying.

To their credit, the Fourth Republic in its last years and the Fifth from the start [6] agreed to sign the Treaty of Rome and implemented it, at least as regards the freeing of trade and the customs union.

But at that very moment, two developments occurred which breathed new life into the concept of economic policy and planning which had originated with the early postwar period. The first resulted from the increased competition which inevitably occurs when frontiers are opened. Even though actual difficulties proved less serious than forecast, many firms proved unable to take up the challenge. Very naturally the governments, which were so close to the employing class, came to their aid, indifferent to the ruinous contradiction between the laws of the market economy and any form of security granted to firms.

The second development was linked to the disastrous mythology of national independence. In order to appear independent, France had to excel in the sector of modern weapons and in industries linked to them. Hence, the enor-

[6] It is natural and proper here to pay homage to the minister directly responsible for the Treaty of Rome, M. Maurice Faure, and to General de Gaulle's first minister of finance, M. Antoine Pinay.

164

mous effort made in the past twelve years for the benefit of these avant-garde sectors.

The economist Lionel Stoleru stresses "the anti-economic nature of this policy which deviates from the objective of competitivity to aim at other targets: ensuring orders for sectors which are in difficulty (naval and aircraft construction for instance); refusing dependence upon America because of political considerations and, because of the lack of enriched uranium, developing reactors based on natural uranium; belonging to the group of nations which possess a 'force de frappe' or are capable of launching satellites, increasing national prestige by building the biggest passenger vessel, or the fastest racing car or aircraft. All these considerations explain why the state has always shown an interest in 'noble' activities which strike the imagination: the atom, space, aircraft, electronics, but has never showed more than minor interest in more 'humble' sectors such as the agricultural and food industries. Dominating the world market for ravioli is not an objective which stirs up crowds, and yet it is possibly a more effective means of guaranteeing employment and increasing incomes than building a prototype unique in the world . . . but which would have every chance of remaining so. More humility and realism would greatly serve the cause of industrial development."

All these policies mean that public effort aimed at stimulating development tends to introduce a very serious distortion into our industrial structures. Subsidies for failing firms, which help essentially traditional sectors in which the rate of growth is low, are ill-suited to strengthen enterprises. The deficiencies of such firms lie more in the quality of the management than in the inadequacy of the means of production which is what the state continues to finance. Furthermore, experience has shown that the effort to promote advanced sectors collides with the factor of size. In order to win in this field, you must have not only enormous human and financial resources but also vast markets, which most often depend upon the state. The American federal state has been able to create, through its policy of government-sponsored research and purchases, a veritable artificial market, which is one of the essential stimulants for development. This is impossible for a medium-sized country like France to imitate—though Ministry of Finances would like to do it.

The two policies converge towards the same result. The structure of French industry is characterized by a "head" and a "tail," both of which are not economically profitable and are disproportionate to the size of our industry. It is impossible to overestimate the seriousness of this situation. According to the diagnosis of American experts, it is probably the most serious problem facing French industry.

Those enterprises which cannot lay claim to public solicitude because they operate properly and even excellently see their development hamstrung by a whole series of factors, the main one of which is the malfunctioning of money markets. Growth requires money. To find it, an extensive money market is required. Of course, the biggest French undertakings have been able to address themselves to the international market. But they are few. The others, especially those in sectors of rapid growth, are unable to finance their own development, owing to the excessive demands the state makes in the money market, either for its own needs or to assist privileged sectors. Thus, the new policy being implemented to finance the telephone system and new motorways in France will, during the next two years, hamper in a particularly dangerous way the growth of the most dynamic enterprises, especially those of small and medium size.

This phenomenon becomes even more serious when enterprises of a family nature are involved. Their owners do everything, beginning with slowing down their growth, to avoid increasing their capital, for this would mean they would lose their majority holding.

This process stands in singular contrast to other countries. In Germany, or Benelux, for example, not only is the money market sufficiently liberalized to allow both growing firms and new businesses to find the resources for continued development, but specific and effective action is undertaken in favor of small- and medium-sized undertakings, in accordance with the principles of the policy of competition.[7]

All of this helps explain the present difficulties of French industry and the flood of literature on our industry's competitiveness which continues in spite of devaluation. It helps explain the persistence, in the French administration, of old habits dating from the times of *dirigisme* and scarcity, which manifest themselves in the distortion of financial circuits, the preservation of privileged circuits, the Treasury calendar, and subventures of all kinds. The very extent of these problems reinforces a natural desire on the part of the administrators that the state should intervene to help undertakings as soon as these are faced with serious difficulties.

They have led to a concept of planning in which it is the business of the state, if not to take the place of the entrepreneur, to tell him which are the sectors of priority development and what growth rates he should reach! Despite all appearances, this is the same old *dirigiste*, quantitative and sectorial conception (of which the "professional plans" are a particularly significant illustration) which prevails to the detriment of a modern conception, founded upon value judgments allowing profitworthiness and the competitiveness of undertakings to be expressed.

[7] This healthy situation in the German money market goes hand in hand with a rigorous annual tax on wealth. This should give cause for reflection to those who will accuse us of injuring the French money market with our radical reforms.

The Future of the French People

We need to adopt an entirely different line of reasoning, including a new and more ambitious definition of the functions of the national Plan. Democratic planning is an essential tool servicing any policy which takes on the dominance of the economy. But taking into account the amount of international competition in a little-specialized, medium-sized country such as France, planning must serve the purpose of systematically pruning away the dead branches of the economy, so the most vigorous ones can grow.

The Plan must express, in figures, the country's choice of civilization. This means especially defining the role of the free market in the satisfaction of various types of needs [8] and evaluating, over the medium term, the size of the collective effort required for the satisfaction of intangible needs, especially community equipment. In accordance with this view, the annual state budget must be conceived, as rigorously as possible, as an instrument of the Plan. The Plan would thus assume an overriding role with regard to public finance.

In accordance with the second point of view, the Plan should be, as Pierre Massé [9] said, an extensive survey of the market at the national level. It should take the widest account of the evolution of international trade and outside competition. This new conception of the Plan demands that all undertakings give the attention required by a modern management system to the planning of their strategy. French industry is particularly backward on this point.

France's economic development should be primarily based upon accelerating the process of industrialization. We lag far behind in this respect. But, for the reasons we have just indicated—international competition and the necessity

[8] See chapter one.
[9] Former commissioner for economic planning (1959–1966).

168

for medium-sized countries to specialize—we must, after having rid ourselves of the prejudices inherited from the past, try to grow in the fields where we excel (especially if these are sectors with high growth coefficients) and in all fields in which we are called upon to excel.

As early as 1955, Japanese planners undertook a prospective survey covering comparative rates of growth in international trade for all main products. Within this overall picture, Japan systematically sought to identify the branches and subbranches where it was strongest.

The logic of thinking in terms of sectors, which is what *dirigisme* and protectionism do, need no longer apply in a medium-sized country the moment it has opted to engage in international competition. The logic which should replace it takes as its starting point the comparative efficiency of individual firms, not of sectors, as well as prospective international demand.

The French possess highly competitive undertakings in many fields: glass, cement, material for public works, public works, aluminum, the motor industry, motor tires, electrical measuring instruments, aeronautics, sporting equipment, alcoholic drinks, and so on.

What means can be used to develop the best firms in these sectors? Laws and regulations? Certainly not. Nor the granting of subsidies: they do not need them. What they do require, and this is the job of the public authorities, is a suitable environment.

The reforms we are proposing to restructure the national budget and grant greater autonomy to local authorities will allow the government to do its proper job, which is to build up the necessary infrastructures in each area of the country, and likewise the powerful incentive to save which will be created will contribute to the creation of a natural money market worthy of the name. This can be achieved by the abolition of the artificial barriers, distortions, and rigid procedures which exist today.

But this is not enough at the national level. To accelerate the development of the economy, to master its operation, there must be a joint effort of all economic agencies. Public information policy can help do this. The mere fact that the public authorities—their authority reinforced by the abandonment of parasitic functions—officially express their opinions concerning these developments is a powerful means of pressure. The "announcement effect" has become a technique of government in the advanced countries, like Sweden and Japan, far more effective than many administrative procedures.

At the level of a united Europe, the capacity for decision which will result will allow the future federation to define and develop a common strategy in those sectors of advanced technology which are essential to economic power and true independence.

The most perspicacious experts are unanimous. Jean Saint-Geours writes: "Really, there is no purely national solution to our industrial problems. . . . With regard to financial resources, markets, and research capabilities the total resources available to French firms—even the biggest ones—are no longer sufficient." Our great ambitions in the field of advanced technology must therefore be implemented within the setting of an organized Europe. All fields in which great technological breakthroughs are impending, fields which are capable of utterly changing ways of life, require the mobilization of enormous financial and human resources, as well as vast markets. This is true of the exploitation of the oceans, electricity from nuclear power, and new means of transport and cybernetics. It is equally true for the software industry, which goes far beyond the mechanics of computers

170

and in which great size increasingly constitutes, as Jacques Lesourne shows, a crucial advantage.[10]

That is the general picture. But if we wish to embrace the socio-cultural traits of France in all their specificity and to make them into a supplementary base of development for the country, we shall also have to attribute a greater part to industries of a very particular type. This idea deserves to be developed because, in the long run, one of these industries is going to constitute the new economic thought of France. To understand this, let us pose the problem in its most extreme form by rereading what Edgar Morin wrote after a long study in the Breton village of Plodémet: "Plodémet is unsuitable for large-scale production, and the latter is unsuitable for Plodémet. This means that if there is an economic possibility apart from trade, cottage industries and the services provided for a resident and summer population, this can only be found in the production of quality goods.

"Now the new demand for 'natural' products of quality which is being created in the urban centers is destined to grow. Here too, the counterwave aroused by the great development of mass-produced goods is complementary to it and will form part of the modern wave itself. This is where the chance of a rebirth lies for a particularly refined type of production in agriculture, cattle raising, furniture-making and preserves—but only on condition that it is capable of integrating itself into modern organization and distribution channels.

"Thus the destiny of Plodémet is not that of a decline through dispersion, its absorption at every level by large-

[10] Jacques Lesourne, the animator, and president of SEMA, the first organization in France for computer counseling, who in 1969 also became president of the OTH, is the living example of what France can achieve by new breakthroughs in the field of organizing intelligence: with his team we are the first of all Europe in software and his branches cover the Common Market.

171

scale enterprise, or the sleepiness of dormitory suburbs. It is going to evolve through the dialectic of modernity."

This dialectic of modernity is one which, if understood economically, can solve an entire range of French problems. It is striking to see our country stupidly allowing activities to decline in fields where it used to be strongest, where it can be strongest, at the very time when the most advanced modern economy was creating new needs in fields which will never stop growing. We are witnessing the decline of our tourist and food industries, which have enormous potential for the future. Crafts involving art, fashion, and creation, in which our reputation is still so great, are being neglected. Everything that is "French" is cast aside, whereas it should be exploited.

France used to be in the very first rank of tourist nations, but for many years her tourist balance has been in deficit. Have we lost sight of the extraordinary deposit of natural and historical resources we have, worth far more than coal or iron on the world market? The French allow IBM and Texas Instruments to teach them it is possible to operate splendid and innovating factories on the Mediterranean coast. We did not discover this for ourselves. We seem unable to see this asset value our countryside has. What a contrast with what has taken place in Italy over the past ten years!

The sectors referred to are not only in full harmony with the national tradition and vocation, but, to refer again to the philosophy of the Japanese plan of development, are among those for which very rapidly growing outlets open every year. They are sectors of most interest to populations enjoying high standards of living, to those equipped with high disposable incomes to whom we can sell for the highest profit. The preconditions for success, however, lie in identify-

172

ing these opportunities and removing the state-imposed road-blocks to the financing of their development.

If we decide to assume our national personality, to revise mistaken conceptions on the economic chessboard on which France has to play, we shall come round, quite naturally, to giving a proper place to "small and medium-sized enter-prises." This expression, in today's language, automatically implies mediocrity. However, the American example—as the tourist can observe along Boston's Route 128, the very image of the future, or on the campus of Stanford University—demonstrates that small and medium-sized businesses are fre-quently those which have the highest degree of profitability in an economy which, because it is becoming more sophisti-cated and diversified, must get as far as possible the utmost output from creativity.[11]

These are the mines to which we can go and look for gold when it lies under our very eyes. The Mediterranean is the cradle of the art of living, the thing the present-day world lacks most. We have inherited innumerable techniques in this field, but we have proved unable to exploit them in-dustrially. One of France's vocations lies here. Folklore? Let us fix a date: soon traditional steelmaking will be appearing folkloric. One rule must be adopted: adaptation. One source of wealth: creation. Soon no others will exist.

This idea, still quite new, fits in even better with our overall plan since it means systematic application of intelli-gence to the creation of riches. We thus have the right to address ourselves very specifically to scientists, research work-

[11] Route 128 is lined with a proliferation of small and medium-sized under-takings founded upon the exploitation of the technological discoveries made in the great universities close by. These undertakings have often been started by university professors or former students. Until the cutback in United States defense spending, many of them constituted fine examples of both contemporary architecture and financial profitability.

ers, and all of those whose working tool is their own brain: you are our inspirers. What we wish to do in connection with the economy is the same as what you have taught humanity as regards nature. The fundamental principle of our political philosophy is directly inspired by your methods of work. If we intend to practice submission to facts, to respect the truth, and to ally ardor with humility, it is because you have demonstrated that this method is the only one.

Many of you are getting very anxious, and you are right. The government has begun to cut into your numbers. We would be lying if we did not tell you this is going to continue. The truth is that research workers employed by the public sector in technology are, for the most part, condemned, sooner or later, to undergo an uncertain reconversion once it becomes obvious that it is impossible for a nation the size of France to continue such a badly conceived effort on the scale it is doing. This effort in the main is pure waste.

Likewise, many research workers working in French firms are doomed to insecurity. Having failed to adapt themselves, these firms will not long be able to sustain themselves in the international competition which is the source of economic progress. Henceforth, there remains only uncertainty, linked to the world-wide strategy of American firms.

It is not without reason that the workers at the frontiers of the mysterious, witnesses of the future, have—better than any other social class—understood that without the prospect of European unity, France is doomed to a stunted destiny.

The innovations emerging from research generally lead to the manufacture of products which have to be sold in a large-scale market to be competitive. Now the market for advanced products is largely dominated by public purchasing. This can be coordinated only by a political authority. Thus, either the political unity of Europe is going to take place, or else many research workers are going to have to choose between crossing the Atlantic or changing their jobs. This would really be a sin against the Holy Ghost, because, increasingly, economic development will be founded essentially upon "second materials," which are the pure creations of the mind.

There are two main types of intelligence: analytic and synthetic. Synthetic intelligences make good generalists. Many Frenchmen are like that. American experts stress that France is very fortunate in having a type of manager (which they take from us every time they can) equipped with great aptitude "for mastering complex problems." For this reason, for several years now, one of the trends of education in the United States consists of training fewer and fewer specialists and more and more generalists. The French are therefore, for France, the richest of raw materials.

Three other factors are going to help us in this respect— the first is the rapid rate of development of research activities. Invention today is often born at the common frontiers of two or more different sciences. An excess of specialization thus often leads to sterility. This explains the multiplication of interdisciplinary teams in laboratories and research centers and underlines once again the importance of the generalist.

The second is that pure sciences, and mathematics especially, are gaining increasing importance in industry compared with applied sciences. Some great companies maintain teams of pure researchers, working in accordance with methods, not by directives. The French have always appeared relatively well endowed to adapt themselves to this manner of working.

Finally, there is no doubt that the industry of knowledge, founded upon information systems and their methods of utilization, is going to grow most rapidly in the near future.

France already occupies a promising place in this respect, as illustrated by SEMA (Society for the Study of Applied Mathematics).

A whole set of assumptions and probabilities thus allows us to claim that France has a particular vocation in the new fields of intellectual activity. It shows the full importance of our proposals concerning education and especially the effort required to bring about the awakening of intelligence.

Thus, whether we refer to tourism, industries of creation, or the industry of knowledge, all these activities have one common characteristic. They suppose geographic locations in regions in which life is most agreeable, thus largely escaping the requirements of Megalopolis. Thus we see the possibility, within the postindustrial perspectives, of multiplying in France both small and medium-sized enterprises with high coefficients of creativeness and small and medium-sized towns built on a human scale, in conformity with town planning adapted to our "policy for life," that is to say, designed for man.

Today the region of the world in which the standard of living is the highest, and research towards different ways of postindustrial ways of life is the most advanced, is California. It lacks any sort of classical industrial resource. Its development is based essentially upon its climate and the creativity of those who decided to settle there. This is the land of the Rand Corporation, Berkeley University, electronic and aerospace industries—all built essentially upon gray matter, on the flexible, rational, nonmaterial organization of teams of brain-workers. No more pit faces, mechanical chains, and hard manual labor leading to exhaustion and degradation. This is the new "farewell to arms" in the era of industrial combat. . . .

California has many social and environmental problems. It

is perhaps not coincidental that its divorce rate is one in two. But California is eternally the land of hope, and what is rising there, under the sun, is hopefully a land of men in which life will be good for all.

Yes, the longer we work on an economic plan for the future of the French people, geared to daily life, the more clearly we see that France today has everything needed for it to become the California of Europe.

TEN

Those Who Suffer Most

As all great military leaders know, the morale of an army depends first and foremost on the care it takes of its wounded and the risks it assumes in order not to abandon them. So does the quality of a policy. That is precisely why the future of all French people depends, first and foremost, on what is done for the weak, the crippled, the disabled—all those who are laid low by our society.

They do not vote very often. They will doubtless hear nothing about the Radical Manifesto. This silent group is made up of those who do not even believe in the possibility of progress, so much have they been cheated in life, and for so long: the forgotten old people, the physically handi-

178

capped, the foreign workers, the enormous mass of the unfortunate; those who have nothing to hope for, except death,
from a policy of mere management; those who are neither
organized, nor trade-unionized, nor supported by anyone;
finally those who, in their moral malaise, are led by their
solitude to ring up the speaking clock on the telephone to
hear something which sounds approximately like a human
voice. Millions and millions of men and women, similar to
us, except that as regards the economic life (and we call it
"life") of the country, they no longer exist.

It is they who interest us most, and foremost. Our society
will be judged not only by its average income per capita,
surely not by its access, or otherwise, to "atomic dignity,"
but according to how it deals with the weakest.

The rulers of Sparta used to force some of their slaves to
get drunk to implant disgust for drunkenness in their children. These slaves were known as Helots. Capitalist law
wishes to have its own helots. If the political system continues to care so little for the "unmentioned," it is because
here too political power is only the auxiliary of the economic
system—even in its cruelty. The economic system requires
that the abject fate of society's rejects should serve as an
example to the others. These pariahs strengthen the arro-
gance of the victors in the social competition. And the more
rigorous competition becomes, the more their numbers increase. Pauperization is a marked tendency of our society.

America is the prime example, but at least Americans have
become aware of it, and their best political minds have been
alerting opinion to the consequences of poverty. France has
opted for the American "old model." We Radicals will take
our inspiration from the examples of Sweden and the Netherlands.

Our aim is to assure full citizenship to all these marginal
people who have fallen by the wayside of the economic

179

motorway. We wish to ensure to every man and woman living in France a guaranteed minimum of resources corresponding to what the American radicals call the negative income tax. With free movement of workers within the Common Market, this measure will naturally have to be extended to the whole of the European community. Who would refuse this?

In addition, the reform of the social security system, already described, will help transform the fate of the "unmentioned." Present social legislation only grants benefits to workers in regular employment whose periods of unemployment or sickness do not exceed certain limits. It is toward the others that the solicitude of society will be shown as a priority measure. Precisely because we are concerned first of all with the fate of those others, HLM allocation offices will be reorganized by municipalities with Radical majorities in order to serve their true purpose. Our objective is to eliminate entirely all the *bidonvilles* ("shanty towns") in those municipalities within ten years.[1]

Finally, we shall undertake to give a new lease of life to the ancient institution of people's tribunes. A Court of Freedoms will be created, so that any citizen injured by an arbitrary decision of government can defend himself quickly and effectively. A social assistance system, which would be part of the proposed students' civic service, will be placed at the disposal of the poorest to help them get assistance.

Next to the "unmentioned," in the order of scandal, comes the working class. No one will deny there has been an in-

[1] M. Michel Debré, with whom we disagree on almost everything, deserves credit for having voted a law in 1964 destined to facilitate the expropriation of land on which *bidonvilles* are built, in order to reconstruct and rehouse the population. This text produced satisfactory results. But as the old *bidonvilles* disappear, new ones are created, often of the clandestine dormitory type. The reception of foreign workers remains badly organized, if not nonexistent.

crease in the standard of living of French workers since the last generation. But it is enough to refer to the mortality figures to see that the French remain divided into unequal races up to the moment of death. Between 1955 and 1960, the mortality rate for every 1,000 inhabitants aged between forty-six and fifty-five varied by 100 per cent according to socio-professional categories: about 60 per 1,000 for technicians in the private sector; 100 per 1,000 for workers and rural wage earners; and 130 for laborers.

These figures merely measure, in overall terms, the burden which the present economic system lays upon the working class. At all times and in all places, the worker must adapt himself to the requirements of the machine. Far from seeing to it that work is defined in terms of human needs and capacities, jobs are first created, and workers are then recruited for them, the workers being compelled to adjust themselves to conditions producing the greatest profits.

The ruling class continues to treat manual labor as servile work, in the exact meaning of the word. It believes that any academic or professional qualification, however slender it may be, gives one a right to employment better paid than manual work.

It is therefore proposed that the Radical Party pledge itself, within a period of five years, to satisfy a basic trade-union demand that the guaranteed minimum wage should increase in proportion to average hourly wages. Finally, as part of a long-term plan, we shall reduce the spread of salaries by increasing the minimum at a higher rate than the increase in average wages. Our objective is, in one generation, to reduce the hierarchy of salaries by about half.

Factory working conditions in France, unlike the United States, remain outside the field of collective bargaining. The working class is becoming the ghetto of an insular subculture. The most competent international experts point out "the resistance of the French employing class to any real organization of the workers allowing them to express their own point of view, which leads to an alienation of these workers from their work."

Such a situation helps explain the political dissatisfaction of the working class; a dissatisfaction which, in turn, only aggravates the problem. When unions refuse contracts for progress, progress too is refused. In the long run this costs the workers dearly. About ten years ago, workers' wages were appreciably higher in France than in Germany. Today, on an hourly basis, they are 30 per cent lower, taking into account the monetary adjustments of 1969. We can thus measure the consequences of what is characteristic of French political and social life: the repulsive power of revolutionary ideology has the effect of permanently shifting towards the right the center of gravity of political life; of strengthening an employer's power, which is as ready as the government to use the blackmail of chaos; of removing representatives of the working class from the centers of decision; and of keeping the latter in a material and moral ghetto. There, no doubt, can be found the origin of the particularly serious and painful problems of the condition of the working class in France.

What is to be done? Illusion arises as soon as the question is asked. It takes the form of brandishing the feeble thunderbolts of legislative and regulatory power in a situation where what is primarily involved is a relation of forces, a set of customs, and the factors of the market place. It would be useless to issue a paper decree, reducing the range of salaries by increasing the lowest and reducing the highest, so long as there is not an abundance of manpower on the one hand, and scarcity on the other.

We have suggested how the trade unions will be able to obtain the material means necessary to operate effectively. It will be up to them to employ them as they see fit. A political party is not entitled to tell them what to do with them.

We would simply like to suggest that it is important to negotiate the concrete conditions of a more human definition of job positions.

In our epoch, Europe has succeeded in eliminating unemployment almost completely, but it has been unable to ensure the full employment of each person's qualifications. Welded to his workbench, assembly line, or office the ordinary worker is imprisoned by less intelligent, less interesting tasks than those of which he is capable. First, job specifications are laid down, and subsequently a search is made to recruit the workers whose profile adapts itself best to the specifications. It would be fitting to demand that employers gradually adopt the opposite idea, of determining job positions in terms of the profile of the workers they employ.

Experiments in other countries show that great progress can be achieved in this direction, especially if, throughout the hierarchical pyramid, jobs are built around the notion of responsibility. It is up to the trade unions to require that each managing director, department manager, or foreman should ask himself, about every one of his subordinates, whether he could be doing something more interesting, what he could be capable of doing later on, and what tasks the machine, or an improved organization, could rid him of.

Trade unions should also be strengthened to cope with the long-term task of revaluating, renovating, and rehabilitating handicrafts. The administration of the economy and likewise morality would gain. If navvies were paid their proper wage, we would never again see the streets of Paris torn up with picks and shovels to find a gas leak and then restored to their initial state by the manual filling-in of the empty trench.

The Radicals will put an end to the practice of constantly invoking Europe as the excuse for refusing social reforms. This alibi consists in saying that social progress goes counter to the requirements of competitiveness within the Common Market. But one of the first effects of European political unity will be to allow the member countries to free themselves, in large measure, from the social shackles involved in their separation.[2]

Also, the worker's trade unions are most often isolated. That is why the Radical Party will help in the creation of *comités paritaires* ("committees in which both sides are equally represented") through which collective conventions could be drawn up. Signatory trade-union organizations at the European level would pledge to get them incorporated under their own national law or practice. French workers, in particular, have everything to gain from this: they have the longest working hours, an average of 45 hours a week against 41 hours in Germany and 39 hours in the United States.

After the "unmentioned" and the workers come the great majority of artisans and shopkeepers, who stand in the front line of suffering and daily insecurity. Their problem is least well known because only recently has it been discovered. It would be rash to claim to present here anything other than some provisional observations and general lines of approach. One can see, nevertheless, that the relations and the links between the problems of the different professional categories are numerous and strong enough to allow the principles of Radicalism to achieve results comparable to those which can now be expected in agricultural matters. This will form the subject of a more detailed policy to be described in the next and last chapter.

[2] In particular, by freeing each one of the member countries from the shackles of the external balance of payments. The overall balance of payments of the European Community, taken as a whole, has been in surplus for over twelve years now.

Napoleon saw England was "a nation of shopkeepers," but today the reverse is true. There are too many shopkeepers in France. Their relative superabundance can be largely explained by the fate of manual workers in France. A young man who has not received any vocational training or an adult who desires to change his job has hardly any choice. They have to become either manual laborers or shopkeepers. They are more likely to choose to become shopkeepers, and this is understandable. The problem is a general one. It is the entire condition of low wage earners which is involved here.

Another characteristic link is the one which, in rural areas, makes the prosperity of the small shop depend on the standard of living of small peasant-farmers, because the big farmers easily drive to the supermarket. Our proposals concerning agriculture will be, in this respect, very important indeed for shopkeepers and artisans in a great number of the French provinces.

The ruling class shows the same prejudices toward these groups as toward the peasantry. Both are considered as mere archaic survivals of a former age. That is why the same theories and attitudes which have outraged the peasant would tomorrow provoke a revolt of the shopkeepers and the artisans.

The well-known amalgam between the big farmers and the small peasants is seen here once again, as we saw it in connection with the painful affair of financing the social security system. The problem would have been solved if the groups involved had applied the Radical principle: capitalist shopkeepers in the future will not be allowed, any more than large salary earners, to benefit from social security unless possibly to cover the most extreme risks.

The Radicals will also abolish the VAT (Value-Added Tax) at the retail stage. This is the tax that adds 23 per cent

185

to the cost of everything except food, wine, clothing, and other staples. It is unnecessary to comment on this decision to underline its importance. VAT at the retail stage possesses very serious drawbacks: there is an enormous amount of paperwork and great encouragement to fraud. Furthermore, it leads small shopkeepers to believe that if they are in difficulties, it is because of the overload of taxes which they sincerely imagine to be a heavier burden for them than for the large stores.

The very limited loss in receipts resulting from this reform can very easily be remedied, either by slightly revising VAT rates or by imposing another local tax, making clear that the option in favor of VAT will also remain open to retail shopkeepers.[3]

Furthermore, implementing our principle of economic security, the Radical Party proposes the extension to shopkeepers and artisans of existing social measures destined to encourage the professional mobility of farmers. There exists a FASASA (social action fund to develop agricultural structures). We shall create a FASASD (social action fund to develop distribution structures). With the same aim, the SAFERs (land-improvement and rural-equipment societies) play a useful part in restructuring farming properties by exercising a right of pre-emption. The Radicals propose that the community should purchase their stalls or shops from the artisan and shopkeepers who, by making an effort to change trades, help to improve the structure of employment and the general level of productivity. On the same lines,

[3] The abolition of VAT at the retail stage will mean a loss of only 3.5 per cent in receipts for the state. Furthermore, it has been noted that in our Common Market partners, the extension of VAT to retail trade is meeting much resistance. For the time being, Italy is refusing to generalize it; Belgium has requested further time before its implementation. As for the Federal Republic, it has provided for a system allowing small shopkeepers to make a choice. This is wise.

186

an annuity will be granted to the oldest among them, if they choose to cease operating.

The overall aim of these measures is to extend individual freedom of choice. It is up to the state to introduce technical assistance and support for cooperation between shopkeepers, similar to what it must undertake in agricultural matters. These proposals must be understood as the expression of a choice of civilization on the part of the Radicals. "The abandonment of cottage industries is just a mistake on the part of the capitalist system," Alfred Sauvy points out very legitimately. "A doctrinal error: the mythology of the machine leads to the belief that these are doomed crafts. An error of training too, because the craftsman ought to be a highly cultivated man. But the bourgeois aversion to manual work has discredited indispensable and high-quality crafts. Unlike the factory worker, the draftsman does not suffer from alienation. He sees the end product of his work. Practically alone in society he preserves his full freedom. Whether he wishes to go on holiday on Friday or work fifty hours when there is much to be done, no one can hinder him. There goes the freest man in society. And yet, these jobs which are so desirable are increasingly being neglected. That is why what we call progress leads to a situation in which the surgeon is often forced to spend his spare time as a plumber."

The solutions proposed above are remedies; they are not a panacea. On the other hand, we see too prevalent in France a certain corruption of the public mind, maintained by the demagogy of professional politicians, which asserts that everyone can both enjoy the benefits of growth and preserve his existing situation as a vested right. We shall not fall into the error of economic Malthusianism. We shall take restrictive measures of a regulatory or fiscal nature against supermarkets and other forms of industrialized distribution. This is an affair of economic freedom.

The Future of the French People

Crushed by the mechanic brutality of the industrial era, the small shop, the craftsman's booth, have re-emerged as witnesses of the new freedoms of postindustrial society. There is no longer a single butcher's-shop in the entire city of Stockholm. But in the "new town" of Columbia, near Baltimore, the most futuristic achievement of America in town planning, one finds plazas surrounded by a whole series of shops, including a dairy which sells a wonderful variety of three hundred French cheeses. There lies the human—that is to say the intelligent—future of commercial activity. Before condemning the grocer or the pork butcher to become laborers, doomed to the bleakness of the HLMs and the suburbs, it would be good to take note of these significant developments. Those who continue to believe in the uniform, subdivided, gigantic, and sad images of industrial society which have been engraved like an unending curse on modern times by Charlie Chaplin's films should take the time to re-educate themselves.

While the profit margins of the small shops are certainly higher, the quality of the service they give and the length of time they remain open are advantages which are appreciated at their proper value in good, economic bookkeeping. In the name of what is it desired to refuse people the right to choose oranges from a display and to argue with their butcher? This is worth a lot to them; therefore it must be paid for.

ELEVEN

Agriculture, Sector
of the Future

There now remains, if we dare say it, the great affair, the one which involves our future as Frenchmen in some of its most essential aspects: the country's agriculture.

Since about five years ago, this problem has been posed in new and now dramatic terms. Despite the rapid decrease of the agricultural population, overproduction tends to increase every year. France is experiencing the kind of agricultural revolution the United States went through fifteen years ago, in which fewer farmers, with more of the tools of science, could produce many more goods.

The standard of living of a considerable number of farmers remains close to an intolerable level of poverty, while the financial sacrifices of the community in favor of agriculture, having doubled in three years, are reaching the limits of the tolerable.

On both sides, the situation is becoming explosive. Most proposals advanced tend more or less in the same direction: toward the disappearance of those external nuisances, the peasants.

From a purely economic point of view, there *are* too many farmers in France. The excess does not have to be calculated in comparison with other countries. The main point is that, thanks to modern techniques, we can achieve the same volume of production on our territory with the number of hands reduced, possibly by half. The remainder represent a sort of concealed unemployment.

Secondly, it is inaccurate to say that average income available per head in agriculture is appreciably lower than that of the other categories of the population put together. Allowing for slight statistical errors, which, though important in these matters, remain limited—farmers are, on average, on a par with national level. This sheds an entirely new light on the agricultural problem for us and for the peasants, because the mass of peasants is really living at the limits of poverty. If parity is achieved, it is only because some farmers enjoy very high incomes, some of them prodigiously high.

These facts lead us to one essential conclusion. Agricultural policy so far has had only two reasons to justify its existence. The first has been to normalize the price of certain products (wheat and butter especially) in cases where world prices are falsified by dumping. The second and more important is of a strictly social nature: to guarantee a minimum income to the poorest peasants.

But French agricultural policy has mixed everything up. The public authorities—that is to say the taxpayers—have in recent years made an enormous financial effort in favor of agriculture, not only in price guarantees, but in a considerable increase in budget allocations for community rural investments, in favorable—and arguable—terms for agricultural credit, and finally in social security measures largely financed by the other sections of the population. But since the basic principle of this policy is to deal in the same way with the industrially organized agriculture in Beauce and the mini-peasantry in the Corrèze, the results defy social objectives.

This situation is due either to the fact that political and economic power go hand in hand, leading to policies which automatically satisfy the privileged, or simply to a lack of foresight. It is difficult to say which. There is no field in which government policy has been more arbitrary, more changeable, or more docilely implemented than in agriculture. The farmers were told: produce wheat! They did. Then they found themselves reproached for producing too much. Nevertheless, the price of wheat is kept at such a level that good farm management demands they should keep producing still more.

The farmers were then told: produce milk! They produced milk. And then they were reproached for producing too much. But the prices quoted for beef, compared with production costs, are such that in most regions milk remains more profitable.

The farmers were told: modernize yourselves, buy tractors! They did so, but after they had completed their modernization, many found themselves ruined; and they are told that it is their own fault.

It was announced that outlets in the Common Market would be unlimited, so they organized themselves for export. They succeeded very well in this. Fortunately, no one remembered to warn them that imports, too, would be unlimited and take a great share of their markets.

Finally, an effort was made to develop agricultural education at the precise moment when it was decreed that agriculture no longer had any future and that the peasants had to quit the soil. Docile unto exile, they left the farms at rates higher than the forecasts.

Will they remain docile to the end, dying silently?

The problem of agriculture is the most French of the problems of France. If the agricultural world is suffering, it is because it is the microcosm of the most violent confrontation between the contradictions of our political heredity and the absence of any coherent plan for a future which will be our own.

Despite a certain evolution, especially as regards regional differentiation, official thought in agricultural matters remains underdeveloped. It resembles what authoritarian regimes apply to the industrialization of Black Africa. For them, first and foremost, the goal is to have smoking factory chimneys, whatever the cost, because it looks "developed." In the same fashion, the upper French administration is determined that French agriculture, at all costs, should resemble that of the United States. And what costs they have been!

The official postulate is that peasants as such must disappear, because they prevent France from rising to the level of a reduced-scale big power. They intended to industrialize agriculture for very large-scale production. The symbol of the efficiency aspired to is, at its limits, the manufacture of processed cheese on a continuous production line. This is the law of progress.

Obviously, the peasant world does not see things in this way. It can only keep quiet. It does not know anything about these matters; only Paris knows. And for Paris, agriculture is only a burden.

Let us now have a look outside. France's agricultural policy within the EEC has proved, in the famous "Brussels marathons" of which we are so proud, to be dramatic nonsense. We have treated our neighboring countries not as partners with whom we wished to establish a true union, but as penny-in-the-slot gambling machines. The propositions which the French government defended and often succeeded in having adopted apply much better to relatively homogeneous agricultural structures—such as those of Germany and the Netherlands—which are essentially based upon small farming, than to an agriculture as differentiated as ours by regions and types of farms.

French political policy today disregards three essential facts:

1. Progress, in the case of food, is an ambiguous notion. In many cases standardization of products is obtained only with the loss of their edible qualities. No knowledgeable consumer would prefer a factory-farm chicken, whether or not hormones are used to raise it.[1]

2. The entire evolution of the contemporary economy is towards constantly increasing differentiation of products in

[1] The use of hormones is banned, but this prohibition is not respected. In an impressive survey published by *Le Monde* in January 1970, Dr. Claudine Escoffier-Lambiotte denounces a "veritable blackmarket of so-called veterinary products in which peddlars distribute widely either amphetamines (or dangerous stimulants—inscribed on List B—used in stud-farms), or implantable hormones (estrogen) whose use is nevertheless forbidden, or even medicines which cannot be used on human beings." She stresses "the seriousness of this gap in the public health protection network which distinguishes us in the most regrettable way from all other countries of Europe." And she concludes: "The scandal, because scandal it is, is of political origin, and we must unfortunately observe that the only reason for this dangerous, prolonged and most surprising neglect lies in the power of material interests, both concentrated and diffused, which is at stake in this affair." Another example, as if any was needed, of the confusion of political and economic power in France.

order to fulfill the specific requirements of each class of clientele; the requirements, particularly of those who possess the greatest amounts of disposable income and who naturally seek out products which are original, unusual, natural, and, if possible, gastronomical.

3. In this respect, France possesses the most extraordinary deposit of food resources in the world. The snobbish elites of all the most highly industrialized countries dream of cognac, champagne, the fine vintages of the Bordelais or Burgundy, and the foie gras of Périgord or the Landes.

Yet in the face of these facts, natural legislation prevents the extension of the best vineyards. Official policy bitterly persists in organizing the disappearance of many farms, at the very time when farm products of high added-value are coming into great demand.

If France were really a democracy, the farmers' representatives would demand to know why the government should find it necessary for American economic experts to come here and ascertain that "taking account of the exceptional comparative advantages of agriculture, compared with those of other countries, French exports of food products are very inadequate." This is directly due to the obstinate prejudices of the administration.[2]

Official policy is drawing up plans for reform, according to which farms of less than 120 hectares and stables with fewer than eighty cows would be eliminated. This is the long-term view! But what is really represented by a productivity rate growing, for a generation, by 6 to 7 per cent a year? Remembering that in the past all such forecasts have always been exceeded, can one measure correctly the increase in production which would be achieved by the implementation of this project? And even rarer are those who include in their reasoning the incidence of technological progress.

[2] Report by Professor Hugh Scott.

Agriculture, Sector of the Future

Within twenty years, a considerable part of meat production will be able to be manufactured from soy beans and even from petroleum; preconditioned cheeses, milk, and eggs will contain a heavy proportion of raw materials of industrial, not agricultural, origin. In short, what appears to be most audaciously modern does not give a true account of what the future will be. A policy is being constructed, ruinous for some, cruel for others, on the basis of calculations which are very probably entirely wrong even now.

Following blindness comes contempt. To whom are they referring, those who denounce the obtuseness of the farmers and the demagogy of their leaders? There is not a single sector of French society in which the progress in the intelligence and social morality of individual persons has been so great in the past generation as in agriculture. No other profession includes so many members showing such concern for so long for the general interest. These men, persistently ridiculed and driven away, often offer the model of what the citizen should be, at a time when the citizen has become a rare article.

What will the Radicals do? We cannot make rash promises. We know that nowhere in the world are agricultural problems being solved satisfactorily. American policy itself, which has been very well analyzed by Roger Priouret, is very much open to criticism. Over 50 per cent of American farm workers have an annual income of under 2,000 dollars a year. The poverty threshold in the United States is estimated to be 3,000 dollars a year. On the other hand, 16 per cent of all farmers receive 72 per cent of the profits from agriculture and have an annual income of more than 10,000 dollars. Furthermore, while the United States does not know what to do with primitive products, such as wheat or rice, it remains an importer of more elaborate products, such as meat and fruit, the consumption of which is increasing.

Yet, whatever the difficulties of this problem, we can nevertheless achieve better results than those being obtained in France today. It has been suggested by Michel Debatisse, in the name of the farmers, that the state should commit itself, by contract with the agricultural profession, to grant it for a period of five or ten years a total amount of financial support, fixed in terms of the increase in the national income. This proposal is not absurd. The amounts involved would probably be put to better use by the farmers themselves than they have been by the state. But we can go beyond this. The Radical program will be drawn up on the basis of two essential principles whose bases have been outlined previously.

The first is to distinguish between techniques of intervention, according to whether they pertain to economic or social action.

Economic techniques are, by their very nature, unsuited to achieve an objective of a social nature. This is as true in agriculture as in everything else. We have seen this proved in the housing queston: blanket aid results in giving the same advantages to the poor man, for whom they are not sufficient to allow him to house himself properly, and to the rich man, who has no need of them. It is clearer still in agricultural matters, where present policy is founded mainly upon price supports. Twenty per cent of all farmers, providing 60 per cent of all production, absorb 60 per cent of the amounts allocated to price supports. The remainder, four farmers out of five, the great bulk of the peasantry, receive only 40 per cent. The sacrifice the community is making for the benefit of the big farmer represents, at present, six times what it makes for the small peasant-farmer.

In addition, agriculture, which absorbs 15 per cent of the active population, pays only 1 per cent of income taxes. Such an exemption obviously represents a privilege—and a considerable one—only for the big farmers, who benefit from the state budget in far higher proportions than the best paid senior government officials.

Since the Radical principle is that capitalist entrepreneurs have no right to state subsidies, farmers, who are capitalists of the soil, will cease to get it. This reform will allow a considerable reduction in the price of the most heavily subsidized vegetable products. Simultaneously, we will implement a system that would more than compensate the low incomes of the small farmers. To do this, we must solve two problems, one basic; the other procedural. Concerning procedures, it goes without saying that a decrease in the level of price guarantees or supports can only be accepted, even for the small peasants, if it is implemented gradually and is parallel with the creation of direct aids to incomes in their favor. At any time, small and medium farmers must be treated appreciably better than they are at present.

We could draw inspiration from the English practice of deficiency payments but cease linking them to the volume of production. We could also return to the system of quotas—established per family, and not per farm this time. Experience has shown that it was a great mistake to abandon it.

As for the basic problem, France's agricultural policy obviously cannot ignore the European realities. On the one hand, the European Commission insists that prices should be reduced, while opening wide the way towards a policy of aid for certain individual farmers in terms of the requirements of a more harmonious regional development. On the other hand, member governments are inclined towards a less strict policy with regard to agricultural prices. The margins for action in this field are therefore not unlimited. But there is nothing to prevent the French state—and this would be true even in a federal framework—from taking back from the big capitalist farmers, by direct taxation, a part or even all of the subsidies from which they could continue to bene-fit unwarrantedly. It is even possible to create an *ad hoc* complementary tax.

If, on the contrary, the reduction of prices were such as to lead to a reduction of the financial benefits which France obtains from Common Market solidarity in agricultural mat-ters, France would then find herself in a much better position to demand that the financial resources mobilized for this purpose be used to extend this solidarity to other social, industrial, or technological fields. This is the right logic for the construction of Europe, to which our partners proclaim their attachment.

The second principle essential for change consists in ceas-ing to treat agriculture as a single whole and allowing the "big fish" to hide behind the "little fish." We must distinguish between the two sorts of agriculture: the one, which is com-petitive like industry (which obviously has no right to claim any direct or indirect aid) to the extent that its activity con-cerns products whose world prices are significant; and the other, described as contractual agriculture, upon which the main effort of community solidarity will be concentrated and whose incomes can thus be appreciably increased, despite the gradual decrease in public expenditure.

These measures will not hinder the decrease in the active farm population. This remains necessary, as long as it is the result of the free choice of those involved. And this trend is growing, especially because so many young women desire to live in town.

The Radical Party can thus commit itself, during the five years of its government action, to reduce the overall cost the community bears on behalf of agriculture. This not only includes budget expenditure and the cost of tax advantages, but the excessive prices paid by consumers. Starting from this basis, the challenge is, in accordance with the basic principles

198

of the Radical plan, to think of the future of French agriculture in French terms—in terms of the future and in terms of enterprise. To think in French terms is, first of all, to remember that France has the lowest population density in Western Europe, the most varied and most agreeable climate, and, consequently, the greatest possibilities of creating properly developed rural areas. Already millions of Germans, Belgians, Dutchmen, and Englishmen are seeking space in which to live, an eminently scarce article. No other country is in a better position to offer this than France.

Next, it means implementing an entirely new complex of operations for rural development. The global subsidy the state will pay to each region will take care of this. The objective will be to make use of available rural manpower to allow low-density areas to become, if they wish, receptive lands for second homes, holiday centers, and rest centers.

In any case as of now the rural world is already in credit to the rest of the community in this respect. Farmers should be remunerated for the advantage which the community obtains from the work they do spontaneously by their upkeep of the landscape. Indeed, in a properly calculated social accountancy, in the same way that the factory should pay for the nuisances it creates by polluting the air and water.

We should reject the official postulate that agricultural products are bulk goods, like coal, and that demand for them can also reach a ceiling. Highly selective action will be taken to multiply the number of *appellations controlées* and to check their abuse. The finest French products of the traditional type, still unknown abroad, can achieve commercial breakthroughs among upper-income citizens of Europe and America. The most modern marketing techniques will be introduced for these products. A specifically French, neo-artisan family agriculture will thus find a huge field for development.

The protection of the quality of products implies wide use of preservation and conditioning techniques which are still not widespread in France, especially deepfreezing, cryoconcentration, and lyophilization. But if this could be done, innumerable districts in regions which are unsuitable for mechanization as they are propitious for cultivating the art of living could export their products, which are just as refined as the wines of Burgundy or Roquefort cheese.

Finally, customers should be offered products which will please them. Large-scale action, including direct international investment, must be undertaken to sell the characteristic products of French agriculture. Instead of persisting in trying to increase our sales of steel abroad with the help of state subsidies, it would be more intelligent to increase the sales of the growing number of French outlets, markets, and restaurants in other countries which would purchase French products. A look at the contemporary economy reveals that in the preindustrial world of French agriculture, there are vast resources which are eminently exploitable, and often even necessary, in the postindustrial world.

French peasant-farmers, like other French people but more so, lack any reason for hope. If we succeed in showing them that in this field, as in every other, hope comes through proper awareness of the economy of growth, linked with respect for the diversity and the deeply rooted attachments of men, we will not have failed in any undertaking.

Robert Gerekens

We were preparing the conclusion of this rather technical work when a flash was announced on the radio: "Three days after the suicide by fire of a sixteen-year-old student in Lille, another student has killed himself by burning himself alive, this Tuesday morning, near the sportsground of the State Technological Lycée, Avenue Gaston-Berger, Lille. The victim, M. Robert Gerekens, aged nineteen, resided with his family at 3 rue Jules-Guesde, Lille. He died shortly after admittance at the Lille Cité Hospitalière."

The next day, the papers told us that Robert Gerekens's father is a railwayman, a former Resistance hero, a member of the Résistance Fer network.

This evening we read in *Le Monde:*

"M. Julien Gerekens, the father of the schoolboy who

killed himself by fire on Tuesday morning at the Lille State Technological Lycée, this afternoon revealed the contents of a message left by his son before he died. Here is the text of this message: "If I die, do not weep. I have done it in sign of protest against violence, to see Love once again and to draw the world's attention to several problems, of which only a small part is dealt with here (I have not got the time to finish). Here are some ideas. On life: everyone is not born with the same opportunities. But we must respect all that surrounds us. On death: this is a means of protest, on condition that death is desired by a being for himself. One can very well refuse it. On love: a great, beautiful and pure sensation. On God: it is difficult to believe in Him, but He is a harbor for many men.' The message ends with this sentence written in larger handwriting: 'I am perfectly conscious.'"

Julien Gerekens has subsequently confided to us, with permission to publish, a few other notes which his son left behind. Here they are:

"What interested me in life: life for itself, that is to say free, in contact with nature and in contact with others.

"My tastes: I like England, then Sweden, then Switzerland. In music: I rather like folk music, and, among the classics, Bach and the composers for the organ. In literature: Pascal, Voltaire, Diderot, Shakespeare. In painting: Breughel (the Elder and the Velvet), Van Gogh, Van Dyck. I do not attribute any importance to cooking and drink.

"What I would have liked to do: to learn German in addition to English and to acquire greater knowledge. To live with my own means. To fight for the happiness of others. . . . To love life more intensely. To discover the other countries of the world and their customs. Intellectual happiness.

"Why I am giving all this up: I have fallen behind morally so much that I am no longer adapted to my time. Selection is so strong that I shall be rejected. Humiliation acts enormously on an individual and I shall never be able to overcome it.

"What I want for others: an equal right for all to live; freedom and love for the individual; a society no longer based upon money.

"What I ask from those I know: to forget me physically but to endeavor to put my ideas into practice. I implore them not to weep; death is not so sad after all. To those who do not know me: not to judge me hastily but to reflect. Be philosophical: reflect before undertaking. And remember that what is good can be bad; and what is bad can be good.

"War: it is the motivation of war which revolts me. By what right do we make war? By that of a few polytechnicians, administrators, military men, and other persons who in the name of we know not what (the country, the state! allow me to laugh . . .) allow themselves to dispose of human lives. War does not bring any solution to problems. Why has man armed himself so much? He is now capable of destroying his own planet and making it dust. When will men become aware of this? When it will be too late? We must react strongly against this: but without violence. Intellectuals must take this subject into consideration; this is crucial. We must no longer again see hatred; love must appear. Man, make a decision, rapidly. Otherwise. . . .

"The beauty which surrounds us, have you noticed it? Nature forms a harmony. It is not monotonous, everything changes, there is LIFE everywhere."

Yes, Robert Gerekens. . . . And also death, it is true, is a means of protest. But the death of a child will never change this world to which, with many others, you say "you could not adapt yourself." It is the world, Gerekens, which we must try—try—to adapt to man. The means now exist. But the will of men? Shall we find a will?

We shall try to move fast. Your deafening appeal teaches us that it is already late. Thank you.

Paris, February 1, 1970